my footprint

my footprint

CARRYING THE WEIGHT
OF THE WORLD

Jeff Garlin

G

GALLERY BOOKS

NEW YORK   LONDON   TORONTO   SYDNEY

Gallery Books
A Division of Simon & Schuster, Inc.
1230 Avenue of the Americas
New York, NY 10020

First Gallery Books hardcover edition February 2010

Gallery Books and colophon are trademarks of Simon & Schuster, Inc.

For information about special discounts for bulk purchases,
please contact Simon & Schuster Special Sales at 1-866-506-1949
or business@simonandschuster.com.

The Simon & Schuster Speakers Bureau can bring authors to your
live event. For more information or to book an event contact the
Simon & Schuster Speakers Bureau at 1-866-248-3049
or visit our website at www.simonspeakers.com.

Designed by Julie Schroeder

Manufactured in the United States of America

10 9 8 7 6 5 4 3 2 1

Library of Congress Cataloging-in-Publication Data is available

ISBN 978-1-4391-5010-8
ISBN 978-1-4391-5527-1 (ebook)

acknowledgments

Thanks to David Mandel, David Wild, Ron and Tammy Schwolsky, Marilu Flores, Peter Murrieta (acknowledgments only), Andrew Stanton, Phil Rosenthal, Anne Czarkowski, Audrey Baranishym, Jessica Pell, Paul Lehr and everyone at the Pritikin Longevity Center, Terri Trese, the word gazebo, Susie Essman, Larry David, Erin O'Malley, Selena Gomez and all her fans (young people love dreidels), Jared Levine, David Miner, Mia Oliver, Elizabeth Clark Zoia, old west collectibles, and my lovely mother, Carole Garlin.

Everyone at Simon & Schuster, including Louise Burke, Jen Bergstrom, Jen Robinson, Michael Nagin, Kristin Dwyer, and Kerrie Loyd.

Richard Abate—Thanks for making it all happen.

Michael Moore—You are a smart one. Thanks for all your expertise.

Ed Begley—Thanks for the guidance and the kindness.

Jonathan Ames—Thanks for the straight dope.

ACKNOWLEDGMENTS

Tricia Boczkowski—Thanks for making my book the best it could be. You are truly wonderful to work with.

Alison Speigel—With you, I'm prolific. I couldn't have done this without you.

Gillian Blake—All I can say to you is DEAR GOD, THANK YOU. Because of you I'm an author. 'nuff said.

And finally Duke, James, and Marla—Thank you for your love, support, and patience. Everything I do, I do for you.

For my father, Gene Garlin

I'm wide awake
I'm wide awake
Wide awake
I'm not sleeping
—U2

prologue

WEDNESDAY, AUGUST 27, 2008

It's the closing night of *WALL-E* at the El Capitan movie theater in Hollywood, California, and I'm walking with my wife to my car. I may have just seen *WALL-E* for the last time on the big screen. I am more moved this time than the other half dozen times that I've seen it. I still can't believe that I'm involved with such a great movie. (In case you didn't know, I was the voice of the Captain of the *Axiom* spaceship.) I call the director, Andrew Stanton, all the time to thank him.

What is staying with me more this time are the themes. Now they're really getting under my skin. I think about how fat I am. And how I'm always saying I'm going to lose weight and rarely do anything to get it done. I think aloud to my wife. I feel bad for her having to hear me think out loud all the time. They're not all gems, you know. I ask her why I don't do something about my poor health. Am I ever going to do something about it? Ever? My character in the movie, the Captain, realizes it's time to do something. If not now, then when?

Later on that night, as I lie in bed with my mind racing, the full idea hits me. I'll write about it. And just like in *WALL-E*, I'll go green, too. I'll lower my carbon footprint as I lower my personal footprint.

For obvious reasons, I need to have a lighter footprint. I need to lose at least fifty, if not one hundred pounds. As far as my carbon footprint is concerned, I'm a recycler and I'm considerate. Other than that I don't know shit. As much trouble as I have with my weight, I'm much more cynical about carbon changes. I'm a boy who loves his air-conditioning. But I'll suck it up! I'll lose lots of weight while becoming ecologically responsible! I'll write a book about it! A friend once told me about José Martí, the poet and writer who led the Cuban independence movement, who once said that there are three things every person should do in his or her life—"plant a tree, have a son, and write a book." I have two sons, and once I write this book, I'll plant a tree. It's all planned out. It's gonna be great!

1

God bless my wife, she always calms me down. As I'm looking through our mail this morning, she says, "You're going to see something you're not going to like." And I say, "Really? What?" She pauses, gives me a knowing look, and says, "Just use it in your comedy." I start thumbing through the mail. I have received a catalog from the good people at Living XL. It's a catalog for fat people who want to stay fat and enjoy themselves. The message is, basically, "Don't lose weight. No, no, no. All the problems that you normally have with being fat—we've got a solution." How do they know to send me a catalog? Do they have a list of fat celebrities?

I open it up. The first product on offer is a three-wheel bike with a five-hundred-pound capacity. As I look at this contraption, I'm wondering how many five-hundred-pound people are sitting around—well, they are obviously sitting or maybe lying around—but how many of them are sitting around thinking, *I so want to go biking. I just don't have the opportunity. I weigh 450. If only there was a bike that could hold my weight. Then I'd have no excuse.*

Next up, fat ponchos. Because we know the regular poncho is so slimming. Has anyone ever put on a poncho and said, "This is not freeing enough?" I guess the only way this thought would cross your mind is if you're a really fat woman and you're wearing a muumuu underneath your oversized poncho. Poncho and muumuu, sounds like a new cop show.

The next page features a lawn mower–handle extender. I don't know what that has to do with being fat. Wait a second; it must be to allow extra room for your stomach! That's probably it.

Now how about one of those chairs you bring to a kid's soccer game, except this one's got an eight-hundred-pound capacity. How many eight-hundred pounders do you see out in society? It must be for a four-hundred pounder, who's got a four-hundred-pound girlfriend who wants to sit on his lap. How about a 650-pound-capacity sand chair. How many 650-pound people do you see at the beach? Do you ever? No! They're at home. They can't leave.

What else? Okay, here's a hammock with a six-hundred-pound capacity. Now, I don't care what you weigh, getting on and off a hammock is quite difficult. I don't care if you weigh 150, hammock mobility is hard for everyone. So you're six hundred pounds. The odds of you getting on that hammock are so slight. You're going to be on the ground. You're six hundred pounds—once you do get on you're never getting off. So it's good that it supports your weight, because you're never getting up again.

Let's see here, next is the big key computer keyboard.

Because Lord knows, your fingers are so fat, a typical computer keyboard's not going to work for you.

Here's one with a great name. It's the Pride XL Mobility Chair. I read the description and learn that when you press a button on the chair, instead of having to get up, the chair lifts you up. And yet they call it the *Pride* Mobility Chair. I think one of the first things about being a proud person is that you can stand up on your own. I'm not talking about someone in a wheelchair or someone who was in an accident. I'm talking about when you really don't have a reason for not being able to stand up yourself. They should call it the Embarrassment Mobility Chair. Or the You've Hit Rock Bottom Mobility Chair. Or even the You Should Be Ashamed Mobility Chair.

Next up is something you've probably seen in commercials. And to me, this is so horrible and wrong . . . it's the Living XL Wearable Sleeves Blanket. Now, how many times have you covered yourself in a blanket, and then thought, *I can't get up! I can't maneuver; if only I had sleeves!* It's only a matter of time until you see someone wearing this thing at the grocery store to keep warm while perusing the frozen foods aisle.

My God, they've got toilets! All right, here's one: a toilet seat that's called the Big John toilet seat. And if you think I'm making this up, I'm not—1,200-pound capacity. Can a 1,200-pound person get up and go to the bathroom, let alone sit down and read? Twelve hundred pounds?! Who's taking a shit in that house? It's described as "durable and convenient." I understand the need for durability on this one, but what makes it more convenient than other toilet seats? Oh, right, it must be for the four-hundred-pound man with the four-hundred-pound girlfriend who wants to sit on his lap as he goes number two—or in this case, number five. The 1,200-pound capacity toilet really takes the worry out of going to the john. Once you get there, there's no panicking questions like, "Can it hold me?" Oh yes, it can. It most certainly can.

And here's another bottomed-out contraption, the "Pistol-Grip, No-Bend Toenail Clippers." Not being able to reach your toes because of the size of your belly—I'm sorry, but that's a low point. Maybe it's not *the* low point. You could be wearing a blanket and clipping your toenails while taking a dump on the Big John. It's a low point just the same.

But here's the moment that might be the real bottom for me: I turn the page and look at the model who's displaying the Cabin Comfort Inflatable Pillow—and who do you think he looks like? That's right, he looks like me. When you're going through a fat catalog and making fun of it, and you get to the last page and the model is your twin, *that's* your low point. It was embarrassing enough just being sent a copy in the mail, but the fact that I look like a model in Living XL renders me speechless. I just don't know what to say. He looks just like me! Wow. I've always wanted to look like a model, but not one from the Living XL catalog. So this is my bottom. Done! I'm not messing around anymore. I'm like the Captain in *WALL-E.* If not now, then when? You will see a weight-loss festival like you've never imagined.

● ● ●

As I get started on this big bowl of adventure, I wonder why I'm doing it. I guess I look at this book as my impetus. My motivating factor. If writing this book doesn't make me lose weight and/or go green, what will?

This might be my only book, ever. I wish someone were writing it for me. Actually, I wish someone were losing the weight for me, too. There are times when I'm happy to sell out. Just not when I'm the writer. If I'm truly responsible for something—and you have to be responsible for your own book, your name's on the cover—I have to make it the best I can. I really hope this book is great. If I do something that's good, I look at it as a failure. Maybe that's harsh, but life . . .

xxxxxxxxxxxxxxxxxxxxxxxxxxxxxxxxxxxxxxxxxxxxxxxxxxx
xxxxxxxxxxxxxxxxxxxxxxxxxxxxxxxxxxxxxxxxxxxxxxxxxxx
xxxxxxxxxxxxxxxxxxxxxxxxxxxxxxxxxxxxxxxxxxxxxxxxxxx

When you see a bunch of *x*'s in a row something happened. Something bad. Bad and self-inflicted. So here's what happened.

I got distracted. I get distracted a lot. I have attention deficit disorder (ADD). That's not such a huge deal—in fact, I think almost every comedian I know has ADD. It's what happens when I get distracted that's the problem. I just went down to the kitchen and ate a huge bowl of Life cereal.

I just had a big bowl of life. Literally. And therein lies the problem.

Let me explain my eating disorder to give you an idea what I'm up against. You can put me in a room. And in that room you have the best pot in the world, the best coke in the world, the greatest glass of wine of all time, and a two-day-old grocery-store sheet cake. Guess where I'm going? Half of it could be covered in ants. I swear to God. And I'd eat the other half. I am an addict. And let me tell you, of all the addictions that are most unattractive, being a compulsive overeater is number one.

Look, if you do drugs, you're going to get laid. Smoke pot? Do blow? Drink? You're having sex. You never hear a woman at a party say, "You see that guy shoving burgers in his mouth? I'm going to fuck the shit out of him. Oh, he is hot. Are those White Castle Slyders he's eating?"

Also, I have a lot going on right now. I'm supposed to hand in a script for a film that I am slated to direct, and I am nowhere near finished. It's no wonder I'm fat. I think I can write a book and a script while I'm in production on *Curb Your Enthusiasm*. By the way, I'm an executive producer and a co-star of that fine production. I figure I should mention that; I never assume that anyone knows who I am. Then again, I guess if you bought this book you probably know who I am and I suppose you like me. If you bought this book and you don't know who I am, then good for you for taking a chance. If you bought this book and you don't like me, then hats off to you. You're the bigger person. Trust me, if I didn't like you, I would never buy your book.

To stay focused, I've decided to keep a diary of my accomplishments, so to speak. So here goes.

THURSDAY, AUGUST 28, 2008

I'm standing in the kitchen staring at a box of Lucky Charms. The magical deliciousness overtakes me. I'll start tomorrow. Although, after I'm done, I'll recycle the box.

FRIDAY, AUGUST 29, 2008

Where did the fresh bagels come from? I'll start on Monday. Labor Day. It's better to start on a date I can remember. Who remembers August 29? I'm sorry if that's your birthday. I didn't mean to insult you.

SATURDAY, AUGUST 30, 2008

No, I'm not starting yet.

MONDAY, SEPTEMBER 1, 2008

I'm currently reading a book of daily meditations for compulsive overeaters (of which I am one). The name of the book is *Food for Thought*. The meditation for today is about being nice to yourself by staying abstinent twenty-four hours a day. I'll keep that in mind. I'd like to make it past one hour without doing damage to myself before I focus on twenty-four. It's 6:00 a.m. and I'm in the kitchen for breakfast. Which, by the way, is late for me. I wake up every day at five thirty. No alarm. No matter what time I go to bed. If I'm not asleep by midnight I know the next day will be a disaster.

So I decide on scrambled egg whites. Opening the refrigerator, I notice—okay, look for—some Pillsbury sugar cookie dough. I eat all the dough. Now I have to run out to the grocery store to replace it before my family wakes up. This brings a level of excitement that I enjoy. Not as much as raw cookie dough, but it's quite enjoyable nonetheless.

xxxxxxxxxxxxxxxxxxxxxxxxxxxxxxxxxxxxxxxxxxxxxxxxxxxxx
xxxxxxxxxxxxxxxxxxxxxxxxxxxxxxxxxxxxxxxxxxxxxxxxxxxxx
xxxxxxxxxxxxxxxxxxxxxxxxxxxxxxxxxxxxxxxxxxxxxxxxxxxxx

Damn. I fell asleep on the couch before I could get to the store. My wife and sons are eating breakfast. I tell my wife that I'm going out to the newsstand.

"Is it open on Labor Day?"

"I think it is."

"What do you need at the newsstand?"

"A fantasy football magazine."

"You and your stupid fantasy football."

A discussion of our different views of fantasy football would not be prudent right now. All I know is, fantasy football just gave me a great cover to run my covert errand, thank you very much.

I pop out to Gelson's and grab my cookie dough and a *Sporting News Fantasy Football* guide. When I get home and roll the magazine around the cookie dough, I drop the grocery bag in the recycling bin.

A quick aside here: yes, I hope to lighten my carbon footprint, because I know it is a big one, but I've always been obsessed with recycling. I'll even take things home from work or social events just to make sure they get recycled properly. The thought of some piece of plastic sitting for hundreds of years in a dump somewhere makes me nuts.

Okay, so after destroying the evidence and replacing the cookie dough, I stroll nonchalantly through the house to make sure I'm in the clear. My children are in the basement playing video games. I can tell it's a Star Wars game by the music. I can hear that my wife is upstairs showering. Actually, I was wrong, because she pops out of our bedroom.

"You're back."

"I'm back."

"Did you get the magazine you needed?"

"Yep."

"I don't understand what's so important about fantasy football that you needed to rush out and get a magazine now."

I shrug my shoulders and she goes off into the shower.

The only living things who saw me put away the cookie dough are my dogs. I know they won't say anything. They love me.

WEDNESDAY, SEPTEMBER 3, 2008

Willingness. Today's meditation is about willingness. I've always been willing to change and evolve. I could also say that I've been willing to fail. I've been ready to eat poorly and avoid exercise. Time to change. I'm willing.

I'm working out with my trainer, Anne, today. I can honestly say, no exaggeration, if it wasn't for Anne, I would not be alive. She's kept me alive. She's really, really, kept me alive.

She can be very serious. Today, as I'm working out with her, I ask her how much money it will take for her to walk up to all the other trainers in the gym and tell them that she's a pretty little ballerina girl. She tells me "I won't, because you couldn't pay me."

"Let's say a million dollars. Would you do it for a million dollars?"

"No, because you don't really have the money."

She just won't go with it. Across the room I see a trainer with huge fake breasts and an attitude.

"See that trainer over there that's taking herself way too seriously? Go over and just pet the back of her head."

"No."

"For ten million?"

"Just focus on your workout."

"What if I said I had the cure for cancer?"

"No."

"C'mon, I'll give you the cure for cancer."

"No."

"Think of all the lives you'll save."

"Stop already."

"What if that trainer got her fake breasts to overcompensate for the anxiety she's feeling from her fear of maybe someday getting cancer? What if you could alleviate her pain by just simply stroking her head? Go ahead and stroke it. But then again, I already have the cure. Why am I waiting to tell you? I should do something about it now. Dear God, woman, I have the cure for cancer and I've done nothing with it."

She stares at me, not even a smile. But I enjoy her nonetheless. I've been with her for nine years. That's amazing . . . and gives you an idea of how long I've been trying to get healthy.

Before I found Anne, another fitness guru tried to help me. When I first moved to Los Angeles, I went to a taping of Bonnie Hunt's sitcom and her guest star that night was Richard Simmons. Bonnie introduced us—yes, he was wearing his signature Richard Simmons outfit (striped dolphin shorts and a sparkly tank top)—and after a brief conversation, he confidentially offered to help me. Confidentially, right! He practically screamed it to the heavens. Reluctantly, I told him I did need help. Nothing had helped me lose weight up to this point. I was a bit desperate. Desperate enough for the magic of Richard Simmons.

Richard asked for my mom's phone number—I gave it to him knowing that her excitement might make up for the second thoughts I was having about this crazy idea—and then he proceeded to call my mom and tell her that he was going to change my life. I would have felt more comfortable if he'd just told her he was going to help me lose weight. He actually could have told my mom that he was going to help me bedazzle all of my shirts, she wouldn't have cared. She was over the moon about simply being on the phone with Richard Simmons. After he was done talking to her, he handed me the phone.

"How about that?"

"You know I love Richard Simmons!"

"No, I didn't, but I do now."

"My heart is beating so fast."

Richard was smiling at me.

"Calm down, Ma."

"Jeffrey, you do whatever that man tells you!"

"Maybe I will."

"Do it, Jeffrey. This is a rare opportunity."

"It is a rare opportunity."

Again, Richard smiled at me.

"Promise me you'll listen to everything he says."

"Maybe."

"Promise me."

"We'll see."

"Not 'we'll see.' "

"I'll try."

"Say it."

"Okay, I'll work with him."

"Please, Jeffrey."

"I just told you I will."

Richard grabbed the phone away from me. "Mrs. Garlin, don't you worry about him. The next time you see him, you won't recognize him."

After making arrangements to meet at Richard's studio, he gave me a big hug and went on his way. He practically floated out of the room. *What have I done?* Really, that's what I was screaming in my head. At least, I figured, I could count on my wife to talk me out of it.

A few days later my wife, Marla, and I arrived at Richard's studio in Beverly Hills. She made me come. And she's not there to exercise. Only to watch my humiliation. I was not prepared for what was about to happen to me. No one could be. Unless you owned Deal-A-Meal and were already dancing away at home to *Sweatin' to the Oldies*. Richard greeted me warmly and announced my arrival to the thirty or so women of various shapes and sizes in the class. We stretched and warmed up to music that probably came from the *Fame* soundtrack.

And before I even knew what was happening, I was jumping around and doing aerobics with Richard and all these women to the song "It's Raining Men." But it didn't stop there. Later, as we bounced along to Diana Ross's "I'm Coming Out," Richard had everyone form a big circle around him. Then he pointed at me to join him in the center. Doing aerobics with Richard Simmons while surrounded by a circle of thirty heavy women in tights—you tell me what word to use to describe this experience.

In addition to attending his classes, I would receive messages on my answering machine that typically went like this: "Happy Monday! It's a beautiful day to exercise! See you soon." I have to admit these messages brought my wife and me great joy. I wish he still called. At one point, a couple of months after I met him, I found myself alone at Richard's house. He introduced me to his dalmatians and showed me his doll collection. (At this point I probably should have run. Run or just decided to be gay. Is there a better time to come out than when you're being shown Richard Simmons's doll collection?)

As I was driving home, I was listening to sports radio. I listen to sports radio all the time, but I'm sure subconsciously I turned it on in an effort to instantly regain my masculinity.

Anyhow, the reason I remember listening to sports radio was that they announced that Northwestern had upset Notre Dame in football. I had planned to watch it on TV that day. But, no, I didn't watch it. Instead, I enjoyed the magic of Richard Simmons's doll collection. I thought, *I can never tell anyone about this.* Until now.

God bless Richard Simmons. He's helped so many people. He tried to help me. I stopped going to his classes after a couple of months. But how would things have been if I'd gotten healthy for good with Richard Simmons? Just imagine the two of us on the talk shows, with him showing me off like Frankenstein's monster.

MONDAY, SEPTEMBER 15, 2008

Today, as a result of the ADD skill set, I'm at the car wash and I've got to be at my son's school for an event in twenty minutes. I don't know why I choose to wash my car minutes before I have to be somewhere. But it's happened before, as if it's some weird habit. I'm supposed to be at an appointment somewhere ASAP, and all of a sudden I'm turning in to a car wash. I should be grateful; at least it's not an In-N-Out Burger.

As I wait impatiently, I see a beautiful Mercedes sedan being hand dried. A very fat guy with long hair and a black baseball cap on backward is talking to the guy who's drying it. The fat guy is getting kind of animated. I'm intrigued, so I move closer and notice a couple of key things. One is that the car has a V12 engine. Second, the guy's baseball cap says SAVE THE PLANET in white block letters. He's got a V12 and he's telling the rest of us to save the Earth. Clearly a conflicted individual. Or one who likes driving cars with big engines and wearing free stuff.

I'm fat, but this fella is a pig. He kind of looks gray. As I make this observation, he lights up a smoke. He's truly a mess. I don't think he's ever exercised. Absolutely no muscle mass. I bet if I touched his arm, it would have the consistency of a water balloon. I can't quite hear what's being said, and now I'm obsessed with figuring out what's going on. I move even closer, and I hear him telling—or rather, ordering—the car-wash guy to put some muscle into it. A guy with no muscle mass should never be condescending to someone who has it, particularly with respect to activities that require muscle. Then fat Earth guy says, "Harder man!" The poor car-wash guy is really working hard. Finally he finishes and hands the keys to fat Earth bozo, who says, "I have no change or money for a tip." He throws his cigarette down, steps on it, and gets in his car. I can't take it anymore, so I say to the fat Earth guy, "That wasn't right. I'm going to tip the guy for you."

"Do what you want; I don't give a shit."

He looks in his backseat, then moves his seat forward and pulls out a stack of newspapers. He stuffs the newspapers into the garbage and gets back in his car.

"What about 'saving the planet'?" I ask. I can't help myself.

"Fuck the planet and—"

I interrupt, "And fuck me. . . . Very good."

He peels out and almost hits a pedestrian. I walk over to the garbage can, pull out the papers, and put them in my trunk.

———

• • •

As I enter my son James's classroom a few minutes late, still obsessing about the ignorance of the guy at the car wash, I receive a swift, angry stare from my wife. A ranger from Joshua Tree National Park is there addressing the class, wearing her full ranger regalia. She seems very serious. This could be a long night.

In a few weeks my son's class is going to Joshua Tree for a two-night camping trip. Two nights in the outdoors. Dear God. As the ranger details the various outdoor activities that my son will be doing, I begin to have an anxiety attack. I'm not a big fan of outdoor activities. I am a big fan of air-conditioning. I hate heat. Heat and hay fever. And touching greenery. I like looking at greenery. But if I touch anything green, I'm gone. I start scratching myself like a crazy man. And, mind you, I don't stop. At least until I've gone home and showered in cool water. After that I'd probably take a nap. It doesn't have anything to do with the itching. I'll just feel like a nap at that point. So sue me. After some time with greenery, if I want a nap that's my business. I also hate spiders and snakes, though I like lizards. They're like little dinosaurs that eat insects. I'm also not a big fan of hiking. I love to walk. But I enjoy walking through a city, not amidst rocks and greenery. I loathe rock climbing, too—I shouldn't climb anything except stairs. And caves, I'm afraid of caves. I'm crazy claustrophobic. Have I left anything out? Oh yeah, the sun. I don't burn easily, but I get rather dizzy if I'm in the sun too long.

I hope I don't come off as too much of a wimp by admitting all of that. Because I'm really not. As a matter of fact, if you put me in an air-conditioned room in some office building in New York City, I'm as tough as the next guy.

The activities my son will be forced to endure include climbing, helmets, and rocks. Apparently they will be climbing under boulders. Under boulders! I run outside to the parking lot for some air, and I feel like throwing up. Minutes later my wife comes out. She is completely unconcerned about my health. Instead, she makes me promise that I won't mention my reservations about the trip to my son. But I know that he's my son (which means he loves the outdoors about as much as I do; I'm not sure he even likes looking at it), and when he finds out the shit they're going to do, he's going to be furious. He's going to want to come home. Oh dear God, I want to save him!

Standing by myself in the parking lot, I realize that I am conflicted about my desire to be green. Well, not as conflicted as that asshole at the car wash. I want to do my part to make the planet cleaner and healthier; I want us all to have a future on this Earth, especially my sons. I recycle religiously—even other people's trash. I know that global warming is real. I know that natural beauty needs to be preserved. I know that I need to do more. But *the last place* I want to go is back to nature. Please don't make me go back to nature. I want to go back to my couch. And then maybe I'll watch the documentary *Planet Earth*. In Blu-ray. I'll see nature the way it was meant to be seen. From my couch.

2

MONDAY, SEPTEMBER 29, 2008, ROSH HASHANAH
(THE JEWISH NEW YEAR)

Oh, aren't good intentions wonderful? I start the day with good intentions. In the morning I eat fruit with some oatmeal—less oatmeal, more fruit. But by the time afternoon rolls around I'm surrounded by way too much food. Apples dipped in honey—apples, good; too much honey, bad. Although eating them on Rosh Hashanah means I'll have a sweeter year. I'm so full of shit. Although it sure would be great if the more food I ate the better year I'd have. God, I wish that were true. I love Jewish food. Trust me, it's good. Ask a Jewish friend to let you know the next time his or her mom makes some noodle kugel. You won't be sorry.

SATURDAY, OCTOBER 4, 2008

Besides my family, there is nothing I'm more devoted to than the Chicago Cubs. If there is a chance that the Cubs could be in the World Series, believe me, my schedule is wide open. I have a Cubs clause in all of my contracts that allows me to take time off from anything I'm filming to attend the Series. None of the studios object to this. They're more realistic than I am. The Cubs are in town playing the Dodgers in the playoffs and I have tickets. If they can win and get to the World Series, it all starts tonight. But as soon as I feel that they are losing and I can't take it anymore, I'll get a cheeseburger. It is the bottom of the first when I get my cheeseburger.

Last year I was at another Cubs play-off game and I thought, *If they win the World Series, then I'm going to change my eating habits.* Well, they didn't even get to the Series; they were beaten badly by the Diamondbacks in the first round. Sitting in the stands at Wrigley Field, as I watched their chance at a World Series win slip away along with my motivation to lose weight, I said to my friend Brad Morris, "I can't handle this. Let's go across the street to the souvenir shop, and whatever team's hats fit us, we'll follow them next year. We'll put the Cubs on the back burner. C'mon how much worse can it be?"

The only team that fit both Brad's and my heads was the New York Mets. I flew back to Los Angeles and was wearing the Mets hat when my wife picked me up. She pointed at my hat and says, "What's that?"

"I'm a Mets fan. Just for one year, I'm a Mets fan. I'm going to go down to Spring Training, I'm going to throw a party for the team, and I'm going to meet all the players. I've decided that I'm going to write a book about my year as a Mets fan and my year losing weight as a Mets fan."

"No you're not."

"Why not?"

"You have two small boys, who have become Cubs fans be-cause of you. They'll be confused that you're going to spend a year being a Mets fan."

Then my wife said her classic line.

"You're not allowed."

So it was over. I was not allowed to be a Mets fan. But I can't blame my wife for putting her foot down; that wasn't even the most absurd scheme I'd devised to provide incentive for losing weight. The most absurd had to do with my son's foreskin. Sometimes inspiration comes from the most unlikely sources.

Both my sons had a bris. The experience is quite unset-tling. Before the first boy was born, I didn't know if we were going to have one. I knew he was going to be circumcised, but I thought maybe the doctor in the hospital would do it—you know, bing, bang, boom, zip in and zip out, Czechoslovakia. But, no. I settled on the bris.

First of all, there is no limit to what you would pay to have your son's penis cut right. But how are you supposed to know if the guy's any good? It's not like you can ask to see samples of his work, nor would you want to, let alone know what to look for even if you could. Let's face it, this is an industry where they could fuck you so bad. They could. "It's going to be twelve thousand dollars, and I'm the only one who does it right." The only response to that is: "Yes, sir."

Somebody at a party told me that he helped out with the

circumcision of his son. He said it was the most moving experience of his life. And I thought, *How dare you?* How arrogant do you have to be to say, "I'm going to join in on the cutting of my son's penis." You can't do that. Can you picture a little boy whose penis ended up looking like a mushroom saying, "Dad, how? Why?"

"Well, son, I joined in the festivities. Someone told me it was a moving experience."

Me, I let the pros handle it. And here's the problem I ran into. After they do it, the foreskin is put into a little foil envelope and you're supposed to take the foreskin and bury it. A tradition I'd never heard of until they handed me my son's foreskin. I couldn't think of any place that I felt a connection to here in L.A., and I'm not going to just bury it in the garden in front of my house. So I thought, *Well, I love baseball, maybe Dodger Stadium?* But that felt wrong; I'm a Cubs fan. So I didn't do anything with it, for the longest time.

And then—somehow—I managed to connect burying the foreskin with launching a new diet in honor of my son. I figured, if I can't motivate myself, this milestone in his young life will do it for me. I want to get healthy so I can be there for all of his milestones. I'll bury the foreskin and there'll be a ceremony and I'll stop eating fatty foods.

But that is not what happened. Instead, one day my family was out of town and I was really lonely without them and I had nothing to do and it was late in the afternoon, and I passed by a billboard advertising Disneyland that said: THE ELECTRICAL PARADE IS ENDING. I'd never seen the electrical parade, and it was ending? *I have to go. I love Disneyland.* And that's when it hit me—Disneyland was the *perfect* place to get rid of the foreskin.

I headed home to get it. It was in my sock drawer. As I was driving, I hatched a plan. I'd go into every land in Disneyland, eat some crap, and as soon as I got through all the lands, I'd dump the foreskin over the side of the boat at Pirates of the Caribbean. Brilliant. My only concern was the possibility of setting off some sort of alarm as I entered the park and having security ask me to empty my pockets.

"Sir, what is this?"

"My son's foreskin."

"What?"

"I'm planning on throwing it in the water on the Pirates of the Caribbean ride."

"Go right in."

So there I was by myself at Disneyland. There were families and friends hanging out and having fun. A grown man alone at Disney is sad, maybe even a bit creepy. Let alone a grown man alone with a foreskin in his pocket.

I started in Tomorrowland with a cheeseburger. I guess we don't all become vegetarians in the future. I went on a few rides. Again, alone. Next, I moseyed over to Fantasyland. I went on a few rides and then it was time to eat again. Fantasyland has an eating area based on *The Hunchback of Notre Dame* or *Beauty and the Beast* or something from that era. Picture a dozen long, wooden tables with people eating off metal plates. Using their fingers. That's what they did in the olden days.

Again, I was by myself, eating a giant turkey leg. I felt ridiculous. I felt like people were staring at me. I had to get out of there—it must be done now.

I got up, went to the Sleeping Beauty Castle, and stood on the bridge with "When You Wish upon a Star" (the original version sung by the character Jiminy Cricket) playing in the background. That was a song that was always playing as I would rock my son to sleep; I took it as a sign. I found a pebble to weigh it down, and I threw his foreskin over the bridge. It went under with a few bubbles and sank out of sight.

Mission accomplished. Sort of. I left, but not before stopping by the Main Street Cone Shop for a chocolate chip cookie ice cream sandwich, so that kind of messed up my plan to start eating healthily after getting rid of my special package.

THURSDAY, OCTOBER 9, 2008, YOM KIPPUR
(THE JEWISH DAY OF ATONEMENT)
Yom Kippur is the most serious of all the Jewish holidays. We are atoning for a year's worth of sins. Part of the way we do this is we don't eat for twenty-four hours. And we sit in temple all day. This will be the year that I'll fast the whole time, and then when I break the fast, I will do it with all fresh and healthy foods . . .

xxxxxxxxxxxxxxxxxxxxxxxxxxxxxxxxxxxxxxxxxxxxxxxxxxx

xxxxxxxxxxxxxxxxxxxxxxxxxxxxxxxxxxxxxxxxxxxxxxxxxxx

xxxxxxxxxxxxxxxxxxxxxxxxxxxxxxxxxxxxxxxxxxxxxxxxx

I am so hungry that I don't even make it an hour in temple. I go to Pink's and have a couple of hot dogs.

MONDAY, OCTOBER 13, 2008, COLUMBUS DAY

I haven't picked up my book of meditations for overeaters in a while. But today's lesson is about honesty and how I should be rigorously honest in all aspects of my life. I think I'm honest. Well, I know I'm not a liar.

I am, however, very stiff right now. My muscles are all tight. Normally I love massages. Not light rubs. I love beat-the-shit-out-of-you massages, the kind that make you pee out the stress. (The masseuse always says, "Drink a lot of water.") People ask how I deal with stress. By getting the crap beaten out of me and then peeing it out.

But I haven't had one in a while, after suffering major humiliation at my last trip to the masseuse. I went to get on the table, and it collapsed. That had never happened to me before. In fact, I've never heard of that happening to anyone. I was just putting my hand down on the table for balance and, boom, it collapsed.

Speaking of boom, on the way down I farted. And what's fascinating about this is that when I went to get on the table, I did not have to fart. I guess that's the body's reaction to collapsing naked. You fart. Also, let me add that falling naked is quite unsettling. So I was sitting naked on the floor and quickly grabbed a sheet to cover my wiener. My feeling was this: She's going to come back in because she's heard me fall, her table's broken, and it doesn't smell so good. Does she need to see my wiener? No, she does not.

I desperately need stretching, so a Pilates instructor that works on my wife is coming over today to help stretch me out. Her name is Audrey and she's a former *Solid Gold* dancer. If you don't know what a *Solid Gold* dancer is, then google it. Even if you do, you should still google it.

Usually my stretching sessions with trainers go about a half hour. This one goes for an hour, and after it's over I feel like throwing up. Number one on my list of things I hate is nausea. Maybe more than Nazis. Actually, I hate Nazis more. I guess the worst thing that could happen to me would be to get food poisoning while in the company of a Nazi. Nausea and Nazis. Not good.

FRIDAY, OCTOBER 17, 2008

Audrey comes over again. She's very encouraging and helpful. But these stretching sessions are making me sick.

SATURDAY, OCTOBER 18, 2008

My wife tells me to pick up the kids from a play date. The family whose house I picked them up at owns the ninety-nine cents store. And they always send crazy stuff home with my children. Well, being close to Halloween, they send them home with pounds and pounds of candy. All it takes is one fun-size Butterfinger and I am off to the races. I wasn't sure why they call them fun size or who they are fun for, but after four or five of those babies in a row, I'm having fun.

If my sons ever catch me eating sugar, I tell them I'll pay them each a hundred dollars. So I eat sugar when they're not around. I've eaten the majority of their Halloween candy for their entire lives, but they've never caught me.

WEDNESDAY, OCTOBER 22, 2008

Another session with Audrey. This time I'm sick and exhausted about halfway through. I tell her that this is the hardest stretching I've ever done. And then it occurs to me.

I ask, "Are we doing Pilates?"

"You bet we are."

Oh well, I guess I'm now doing Pilates.

THURSDAY, OCTOBER 23, 2008

I'm meeting with Lake Bell to discuss the film I am writing and directing. A funny and beautiful actress, I'm meeting her at a vegetarian restaurant—she's a vegetarian. As she orders her food, I think, *Hey, from this moment on I'll be vegetarian.* I'm serious! There are so many reasons to be a vegetarian. Yes, compassion and good health are good reasons. But, also, to be truly green you need to be a vegetarian. Did you know that following a vegetarian diet reduces more emissions than driving a hybrid car? Think of all the gas used to feed and then transfer meat. The water used to produce a hamburger equals the water from showering every day for two and a half weeks. One hamburger! Don't believe me, but I read about it in a magazine. Anyway, I will become a vegetarian today and then Lake Bell and I will get a big laugh on the set about how it all changed for me when I met with her.

The thing is, a few weeks ago, I met with Jason Bateman for the movie. He's a funny and handsome actor who would be good opposite a funny and beautiful actress. We met at a coffeehouse by a taco place, and as soon as he left I had a couple of tacos. Actually, four. After I finished them, I decided that from here on in, I'd start fresh, and, yes, when we're on the set making the movie and I'm in perfect shape, we'll laugh about that day we met and how I had four tacos.

I've been doing this for years, making pacts with myself about last meals. When I was in Second City, there would sometimes be corporate gigs. Corporate gigs basically meant that we would go to a company or a hotel where they were having a conference and do a show: sometimes an abbreviated show, sometimes a show where we would incorporate the names of different people in the company or make a comment about them; you know, that sort of thing.

Well, one of these gigs was at a hotel on Michigan Avenue in Chicago, and we were supposed to dress like gangsters and walk around the main ballroom and mingle with a bunch of insurance people. The woman who ran the thing was one of these crazy, controlling, has-issues-with-everything festival type of people. She was not pleased with me because I refused to talk like a gangster. I said, "No one said anything to me about talking like a gangster. How does a gangster talk? I don't understand how I'm supposed to talk." Other people did versions of gangster talk, but I didn't. So I got fired in the middle of the gig. And when I asked her where she put our stuff so I could change back into my clothes, she pointed and said, "We've moved it into this other room; go in there."

As I opened the door—I remember this so clearly—a Tom Jones song called "Help Yourself" was playing in the background. Little did I know. In the room were all the desserts for a big wedding. Tables of chocolate-covered strawberries, cookies, cakes, little cupcakes. I stood there in shock. I changed my clothes quickly so I could focus on the desserts until I got caught or sick, whichever came first. Then I took one of each and rearranged the sweets on the plates so no one would know anything was missing. Everything was delicious. And the song "Help Yourself" was playing, so it was like a gift. I looked up and said, "Thank you, God, I recognize your sign." The sign being a celebratory one-man dessert festival, signaling the end of gluttony. After this I would eat healthily.

I must have spent half an hour in there eating, until I couldn't eat any more. I walked home, which was a mile and a half—I needed to walk it off. But what I didn't know was that I was prediabetic at that point. I collapsed when I got home and woke up that night really hungry. The first thing I did was get a hot dog at the Wiener Circle. I ignored the sign from God within one day!

And now again, after my first meal as a vegetarian I wait too long to eat and go to In-N-Out Burger for a Double-Double. I guess I'm not a vegetarian anymore. At least not today.

SUNDAY, OCTOBER 26, 2008
Today I have an orientation meeting for my son's bar mitzvah, and I thought, *all right, in honor of my son's bar mitzvah, I'll start today . . .*

XXXXXXXXXXXXXXXXXXXXXXXXXXXXXXXXXXXXXXXXXXXXXXXXXXXX
XXXXXXXXXXXXXXXXXXXXXXXXXXXXXXXXXXXXXXXXXXXXXXXXXXX
XXXXXXXXXXXXXXXXXXXXXXXXXXXXXXXXXXXXXXXXXXXXXXXXXXX

I didn't get to the meeting on time. I probably didn't want

to. Orientation meetings generally aren't fun. Especially at temple. On the way to the meeting I stop off at Du-par's restaurant for breakfast. I say to the waitress, "I'd like some pancakes." I shouldn't have pancakes to begin with. She asks, "Short stack or regular?" I say, "Regular." Short stack means "for a normal person," and regular means "you are a freak of nature." It's a stack of pancakes the size of my head. It's gigantic. By the way, I was by myself in a little booth reading the Sunday *New York Times*. They say that newspapers are going to be extinct soon. What am I supposed to do in the future when I go for breakfast at a restaurant, bring my computer?

The pancakes arrive. They are huge, and there are five of them. I eat almost the entire thing, along with three cups of syrup. This is wrong on every level.

In the afternoon I get really sick, because I haven't eaten like that in a long time. I look pregnant. I'm throwing up. Throwing up doesn't bother me, but being nauseous does. As you know, I have an intense fear of nausea, and now I am so nauseous. All because I said regular stack.

My problem is mostly with sugar. Having the pancakes and syrup will now set me off. A candy bar, ice cream, cookies, a milk shake, and I'm gone. I'll put on twenty pounds in five minutes. But I won't stop eating. It's not good.

FRIDAY, OCTOBER 31, 2008
Today is Halloween.
xxxxxxxxxxxxxxxxxxxxxxxxxxxxxxxxxxxxxxxxxxxxxxxxxxxx

xxxxxxxxxxxxxxxxxxxxxxxxxxxxxxxxxxxxxxxxxxxxxxxxxxxxxxx
xxxxxxxxxxxxxxxxxxxxxxxxxxxxxxxxxxxxxxxxxxxxxxxxxxxxxxx

TUESDAY, NOVEMBER 4, 2008 (ELECTION DAY)

My meditation today is about being satisfied with enough. What is enough . . . when it comes to, say, cookies? One, a few, a half dozen? When it comes to cookies, once you get sick, you've had enough.

Today I will not be satisfied unless Barack Obama becomes president. I leave early in the morning to vote. As I punch in my vote for president, I cry. If *I* feel this way, I can only imagine what an eighty-year-old black man must feel. I only know what it feels to be seventy-nine and black. Don't ask me how. But I do.

After my experience voting, it brings me pause to make today the day I start. On the one hand, it certainly could be a historic and momentous day to begin. However, do I want to do that to Barack? What if all my past failures at getting healthy bring him bad luck? And he loses? I couldn't take it. I might never recover. So I take myself out of the equation and go to In-N-Out and have a Double-Double and a chocolate milk shake.

Later, as I'm watching his acceptance speech, I think to myself, *I made the right choice. He needs a fresh start. He doesn't need the albatross of my weight loss hanging around his neck.*

TUESDAY, NOVEMBER 11, 2008

Over the years I've had major problems with back spasms. I'm thinking maybe I can blame the Pilates and the torture can end. But tonight I have my friend Preston's play reading. He really wants me to come. I won't let him down. God forbid I should ever be that considerate to myself. I guarantee if I were, I wouldn't be in the terrible shape I'm in.

I take a pack of ice for my back and head off to the play, which is good, but the chairs are stiff and uncomfortable. My spasms are getting bad. I'm in a great deal of pain. I leave at intermission.

As I'm driving home, maybe ten minutes from the house, the ice is really helping but I gotta pee. Oh, boy, do I gotta pee. Normally I could hold my pee for the ten minutes and make it home. Not this particular night. No, the pee is not being held in. I'm driving and I can't find a place that would be appropriate for me to pee. So I go up a side street and, damn, it's too well lit.

Finally I find an apartment building with scaffolding in front of it. It's poorly lit, but it's lit. I don't care. I'm about to explode. I get out of my car and I run, leaving my car door open. I barely make it. I'm standing beside a Dumpster about to pee. I feel a light and I turn my head. And behind my car is a line of four cars with their lights on. They can all see me. Nobody can see my wiener, but I know they all know what I'm doing. The weird thing is, why aren't they driving around my car? There's plenty of room even with my door being open. I actually swing my arm and scream for them to go around. They start to move.

I can't wait anymore and I scramble, but I can't get my wiener out in time, and I pee on myself. Not a ton. Some. Enough. After I'm done, I get in my car to drive home.

xxxxxxxxxxxxxxxxxxxxxxxxxxxxxxxxxxxxxxxxxxxxxxxxxxxxx
xxxxxxxxxxxxxxxxxxxxxxxxxxxxxxxxxxxxxxxxxxxxxxxxxxxxx
xxxxxxxxxxxxxxxxxxxxxxxxxxxxxxxxxxxxxxxxxxxxxxxxxxxxx

Here's what happened. I'm hungry. I haven't eaten dinner. I'm not going into some place and saying, "Table for one," with wet underwear. So I go to the drive-through at McDonald's with pee in my pants. I'm an addict; have I mentioned that? I have a refrigerator, I have a family, there's food in my house. But I can't wait; I have to have the burger. A Quarter Pounder with pee in my pants. That's a new one. Even for me.

3

FRIDAY, NOVEMBER 14, 2008

I have decided that sugar must be eliminated from my diet in order for me to function. I've done it a few times before. I know it can be done. It's just so hard. When I'm not eating sugar and I'm eating very healthily, for the first few days of the endeavor I'm not really that pleasant. I'm not *un*pleasant; for instance, I don't yell, "Hey, cocksucker" at people for no reason. But I do have a short window of patience. And when I'm chock-full of sugar, nobody's more patient.

Anyway, I'm doing this Disney show. I do it once a year. It's called *Wizards of Waverly Place*. My friend Peter Murietta runs it, and my kids love it, so I keep coming back. Today we're doing a run-through for the network. I should tell you that Disney tries to be green. Tries. For example, they don't have plastic bottles anymore. Instead of just grabbing a bottle of water, you have to get it from a big jug. But know that the cups they give you are plastic cups. Either do it right or don't do it. (Remember, no sugar makes a man crazy.) They also now print scripts on two-sided pages. Now, I have read scripts that way before, but not when I'm rehearsing a TV show—I need it on one side and that's it. I should be happy that they're attempting to be thoughtful about the environment. But I can't be happy right now—not without cookies. The script supervisor had a one-sided script for me to rehearse with. Being green and being hungry apparently don't mix well. Which might be a big problem for this mission of mine.

Someone has moved my script for the network run-through. So I grab a two-sided script without realizing it and twice in about five minutes, with everyone watching, I miss my lines because they aren't where I thought they'd be. Well, after the second time—at a run-through for a children's show, mind you—I scream, "Fuck Disney!" With the Disney executives there. And as you know, I was in *WALL-E*; I am associated with the fine people at Disney. Foolish or not, the important thing is, I've gone two days without sugar and I can't be held responsible for my actions.

Later that night I do an internet talk show, which is set up in the host's sister's garage. Literally. Don't even get me started. The host is very funny, though, so I'm hoping that he gets out of his sister's garage one day. Maybe she'll let him in the living room. How is it that I get coerced into doing these things?

Actually, I can tell you why, if you allow me a digression. I was on the last three seasons of *Mad About You* and I played a character named Marvin who worked at the sporting goods store. Getting the part was one of the biggest breaks of my career. I remember saying to my agent one day, "Do not send me out on any same-day auditions." Sometimes I would get a call in the morning and need to go in that afternoon. I told him that I needed the material the night before to be able to prepare. Of course, the next day he called and said I had an audition for *Mad About You* that afternoon. I agreed to go but told him that this would be the last one; I'd never do another same-day audition again. Well, I went in and I felt good about it. That's the one thing I always wanted when I was auditioning—to give the performance I wanted, and either they would dig me or they wouldn't. You can't control whether or not you get the gig, but you can control whether or not you are happy with your audition.

Later that day I got the call and they booked me. I was supposed to start two days later, but the next day I got another call, this time telling me my part had been cut to one line. They told me that they understood that this wasn't what I had auditioned for and I didn't have to do it and they'd still pay me. I'd done much bigger parts at this point, but it wasn't like I was so busy or in such great demand. So I said, what the hell, and went in to deliver my one line. I don't remember what the line was, but it was a big joke, and I nailed it. And I also had great chemistry with John Pankow and Paul Reiser.

The producers came up to me afterward and told me that they thought there was something there, and they were going to write more stuff for me. I ended up being on the show for three years. I was even in the finale. They just embraced me completely. And I served no purpose in the show except to come in and be funny. So it just goes to show you, sometimes you've just got to break your own rules, throw your ego to the side, open yourself up, and things happen. You learn something, you get better, you get a break. Who knows? Things happen even now for me, at forty-six.

I can't say that anything significant will come of this garage interview. But they do give me a box the size of my stomach, filled with baked goods, as their parting gift. The host's wife owns a bake shop. Trust me, I'm tempted, but I don't touch any of it.

Later that night I'm at The Comedy Store to do a set. I've got about ten minutes before I go on. While I'm waiting, I sit outside in front of the club and watch the girls walk by on Sunset Boulevard. They're all dressed pretty risqué, and I think, *If one of them were a hooker, how would I know?* They all look like hookers. Every single one of them! And what's amazing is that probably none of them are. If you were to put someone in a time machine twenty years ago and drop them right here, right now, they'd say, "Oh my God, what are all these hookers doing out?!"

Right after my set I walk down the block to one of my favorite bookstores, Book Soup. Artie Lange is having a book signing from ten to midnight. He and I have never met, but we share the same lawyer and agent, so I was able to read his book before publication. Once I read it, I realized that I'm not as fucked up as I thought I was. If you want to see the most honest writing about addiction in show business, it's there. He's addicted to everything—alcohol, drugs, food, and drama. My jaw was on the floor the entire time.

Comparatively, I feel very lucky. Me, I just eat lots of sugar, pee on myself, and go to fast-food drive-throughs to buy inappropriate food at inappropriate hours. But the things he's done—wow. Artie is really funny and immensely talented. I hope he gets sober and has a great life. I hope we both do.

I've never had much interest in drugs. I avoided them. I mean, do I really need to smoke something that's going to make me hungrier? In the late eighties when I first met Janeane Garofalo, she said to me, "I'd really like to do some mushrooms with you." I was really hesitant because I had never done "shrooms."

We never did them. But as time went on, we became very good friends, even roommates for a while, and she turned to me one day and said, "I'm going to tell you something. You're the last person on Earth I should ever do mushrooms with. I don't know what would happen if I did mushrooms with you, but I know it would be horrible. You should never do mushrooms, and I should never do them with you." I could not have agreed more. I've still never eaten mushrooms, or whatever it is you do with them.

I'm scared of drugs. I'm scared if I do blow, I'll die that night. I much prefer the addiction of compulsive overeating, which provides a nice slow death, one that takes a good period of time. You get to see at least your fifties, sixties, if not seventies. Actually, you don't see a lot of fat seventy-year-olds. But it's a much slower death. Blow or heroin . . . done!

Drinking has never been an issue for me, either. My family moved from Chicago to Florida when I was in junior high and I stayed there through college. I was in high school and college in the late seventies and early eighties, when Fort Lauderdale was still the spring break capital and the rest of the year was tropical and sleepy. Now it's unrecognizable. Back in those days I used to drink a great deal of beer. I would get drunk with my friends every weekend. But it never became a problem. I stopped shortly after I started performing in night-clubs in my early twenties. I didn't stop because I had a prob-lem. I stopped because I was now a professional comedian and it would be embarrassing to get drunk at my place of business. I worked nights, and I wasn't going to drink during the day. How could I perform at night if I was drinking? To this day, I bet I average a couple of beers a year. But don't go thinking I have any self-discipline. Trust me, if alcohol tasted like milk shakes, I'd be an alcoholic. I would. I totally would.

The funny thing is, lately I've been going to Alcoholics Anonymous meetings, instead of Overeaters Anonymous. I'm addicted to food; you know that. I'm not an alcoholic by any stretch. My issue is with milk shakes, not with beer. But I've been going to this A.A. meeting once a week because it's so fucking hard-core. You walk in, and there's a purpose. Every-one has the right sense of urgency and importance. I don't find that in OA. OA meetings are attended mostly by women. They talk about the weather; they talk about friendships; they even talk about going shopping with their mothers whom they hate. They talk about anything but food. I don't feel a sense of accomplishment when I'm done, except to say: I sat through that. "Oh, look at me. I sat through the most boring hour of my life." So I'm not going to OA anymore. I'm done. But I'm not done losing weight.

SATURDAY, NOVEMBER 15, 2008

Today we're having a square dance at our house for my son's class to raise money for the school. I hate square dancing. But you know what is really great? At the square dance we're serving that big box of pastries from the talk show in that guy's garage. (That's recycling and dieting at the same time, if you didn't catch on.)

xxxxxxxxxxxxxxxxxxxxxxxxxxxxxxxxxxxxxxxxxxxxxxxxxxxx
xxxxxxxxxxxxxxxxxxxxxxxxxxxxxxxxxxxxxxxxxxxxxxxxxxxx
xxxxxxxxxxxxxxxxxxxxxxxxxxxxxxxxxxxxxxxxxxxxxxxxxxxx

After the party, I'm in the kitchen looking at what is left of the sweets. I only have a little bit of it, and then it's good night. That's what happens; you get buzzed and then you fall asleep. And when I wake up, I feel like I just woke up from a coma. I wish I'd just taken my partner and do-si-doed.

SUNDAY, NOVEMBER 16, 2008

I guess it's pretty clear that I haven't lost any weight since the *WALL-E* screening. I bet you're wondering if I've done anything to lower my carbon footprint since then. And I'm happy to report that I have. In fact, my wife thinks I'm taking it a little too far.

At my weekly Sunday-night stand-up show at the UCB Theatre, I've been giving away things from our house. All sorts of things. Because I have too much stuff. Not enough that I need to rent a storage unit, but still I have way too much. And when you're someone like me, you're constantly being given things. Bags of things. Any event I go to—an awards ceremony, a charity function—they give you a gift bag. A gift bag filled with notions and lotions and iPods and video games. Out of all the gift bags I've been given, I have given away 90 percent of the stuff. Usually to the audience at my show . . . please come sometime; I promise to give you something.

Not only do I give away gift bags, but books, CDs, DVDs, LPs, scripts, candy, Pop-Tarts, and televisions. Tonight at my show I give away a printer. When I give things away, it feels great. Like my house is losing weight. Actually, I feel lighter. But as good as recycling is for my carbon footprint, it's not enough. Tomorrow I'm going to call one of my favorite actors, Ed Begley Jr., who is also the king of environmentalists and a supernice guy as well. He'll help me.

TUESDAY, NOVEMBER 18, 2008

Today was the first production meeting for *Curb Your Enthusiasm*. I wasn't there, but I heard what happened afterward. I recently hired a new assistant, nice fella. At the first production meeting people stand up and say their names and what their responsibilities are on the show. There are usually about six new people every season. So at the meeting my assistant stands up, says his name, and adds, "I'm Jeff Garlin's assistant." The room explodes with laughter. For a reason.

I've had, probably, fifteen assistants in seven seasons of the show, sometimes two or three a season. And I'm always firing them. Susie Essman, my TV wife, recently said to me, "You've been through more assistants than Attila the Hun had wives." The crew has an over-under bet, which means they will set a date, collect a pool of money, and the winner is the one who guesses closest to the date I fire my assistant.

Remember that I have attention deficit disorder, which makes me terrible at hiring assistants—I can't focus and be patient about it. I generally end up hiring people who, for whatever reason, are always asking me what they should be doing. And I, being distracted, need someone to tell me what to do. So we inevitably make a lousy pair. I've had assistants who were intimidated by me and one person who was actually starstruck. With me! At times I have actually thought, *I hired a retarded person* (mentally challenged—I know better—but that's not the word I thought at the time). I've hired people with no work ethic whatsoever. The first day they're asking, "Can I leave now?" I have a reputation not just for firing but also for letting my assistants leave early. But on your first day, do you have to walk up to me and say, "Can I leave now?"

My new assistant seems pretty good so far. Poor guy, he must be terrified after the whole betting pool thing. I'm definitely not going to fire this one.

WEDNESDAY, NOVEMBER 19, 2008

Today's meditation is about knowing the difference between appetite and hunger. I'm not sure I know the difference, but I do know this: I'm always hungry and I sure can eat a lot. It's the perfect topic for today, because I'm having breakfast at the Farmers Market on Third and Fairfax.

The Farmers Market is the greatest place in L.A. It is a collection of stores, restaurants, bars, and of course fresh fruit and vegetable stands, and it's all outdoors. I'm there a lot, weekday mornings mostly, having coffee with a group of friends. The Farmers Market is the most wonderful place to hang out in the morning—it's mostly mellow, though you also get the freakiest freaks—but past eleven thirty, it's over. By noon it's a whole new thing. Lots of tourists. There are plenty of tourists in the morning, but they mostly come from *The Price Is Right*, as CBS Television City is right next door. Their T-shirts used to say WE LOVE YOU, BOB, now they say WE LOVE YOU, DREW. These people make me look thin.

But the bars at the market are what I'm most intrigued by. There are people there at 10:00 a.m. As I'm eating an omelet, they're drinking. We all have our addictions. Except an omelet at ten . . . okay, it's my second one, but nonetheless . . . is much more acceptable than a couple of beers. When you're on your second omelet, no one's saying, "What's wrong with him?" Unless you yell out, "It's my second one!" no one seems to notice.

THURSDAY, NOVEMBER 20, 2008
Today is the first *Curb Your Enthusiasm* casting session for the new season. Today's the day I start!

I haven't eaten breakfast, mistake number one. I'm not at work ten minutes and I go into the kitchen area to see what's there, and they've got all different kinds of cereal, oatmeal, healthy things. I'm an addict who's on autopilot. I look in the freezer first. It's filled with boxes of Hot Pockets. I'm not sure what these are exactly, but I'm guessing they're hot pockets of salt, cheese, and a boatload of artificial ingredients. Then I open the refrigerator and find my pot of gold. Pudding! I am a freak for pudding. So I say, "I'll just have one pudding and then I'll start fresh." I actually say that out loud. I announce to myself that this will be the last one; that way I'll always remember having my last pudding in the *Curb* kitchen. But unfortunately these are snack packs that come in packages of four, and there are two packages in the refrigerator. So I don't just have one snack pack, I have all eight puddings. I realize I'm not starting today.

FRIDAY, NOVEMBER 21, 2008

I fired my assistant today. I don't even want to talk about it. If I criticize him I'll feel worse.

4

Finally, I'm getting my ass in gear about going green. The losing weight thing isn't going so well. At least, maybe, this part of my mission will be easier.

Today I'm going to Ed Begley's solar-powered house to ask him some questions and get on the right path toward lowering my carbon footprint. When it comes to being green, he walks the walk.

As Ed welcomes me into his home, the first thing I notice is that it looks normal. Downright comfortable. I pictured him living in some sort of ecological Wonka world.

"I love that you're doing this, Jeff," Ed says. "God bless you."

Ed is not just the greenest but also the nicest person you could hope to meet. He's the kind of guy you want to impress, but he's hard to impress—because he is so much more, well, impressive than you. We sit down in his living room. A pleasant couch, a coffee table, a couple of chairs. I bet they were made out of recycled cereal boxes.

"When I tell people about this project, I tell them that you're my rabbi, my chinaman," I say. "That's an old political term, you know, as in, 'he's my chinaman.' And everyone says, 'Who better than Ed Begley?'"

Immediately, I'm worried that it's racist to say "my chinaman" or "rabbi." I may be fat and only the palest shade of green, but I'm not a racist! I realize I don't really know what chinaman means. Quickly, I change the subject.

"People have told me that when you were filming *A Mighty Wind* at the Orpheum, you rode your bike to the bus to get to work."

"That's right."

"I would like to do that to get to *Curb Your Enthusiasm*." Biking to work is the perfect way to kill two birds with one stone—I can exercise and lower my carbon footprint at the same time. "Except I don't have a bike."

"You can. You can bike and take the bus, or just take the bus. The good thing about biking with the bus is that you go right from your house to the bus stop. There's no place in L.A. that I can think of where you can't bike a reasonable distance to get to a bus stop. And then they've got racks on every bus in L.A. They're in front. It's real easy. There's a handle, first time you see it you go, oh shit, because you don't want to hold anybody up. You panic, thinking you don't want to hold up the bus, but it's real easy."

"And the bus driver's patient while you're doing this?" I envision struggling to get my bike on the rack. It's not pretty.

"The bus driver's patient. I've never seen one yell, 'Come on! We gotta go.' "

He's never seen it happen, but there is always a first. "And then what do you do, pay with cash on the bus? I've never taken a bus here."

In my twenties, when I lived in Chicago, I took the bus. And then in New York I took the subway and the bus. It's just that nobody takes the bus in L.A. unless they have to. I don't have to. If you were me, you wouldn't want to take the bus. You wouldn't. For me to say, "I'm going to take the bus," in L.A. that's a huge deal. I'll be taking the bus from the Valley to, like, deep in Santa Monica. That's a long way.

L.A. isn't really a place suited to public transportation—everyone has a car, or wants one. I still take the bus in Chicago and New York—my car, being, of course, back in L.A. I take the 151 in Chicago, up Michigan Avenue and Lake Shore Drive. But nowadays when I'm on the bus, people will say to me, "What are you doing on the bus?" It's as if you reach a certain point of success in life, and you shouldn't take public transportation anymore. When I take the subway in New York, strangers say, "What the fuck you doing here?" They swear like that in New York. "What the fuck are you doing here?" But I decide I'm going to try taking the bus in L.A. and see what happens.

The thing is, I still have my car.

"You still take the bus these days?" I ask Ed.

"I do; I take the bus. My transportation hierarchy is walking, because I live in a neighborhood. I go over to the sushi place, the post office, the bank," he says.

"And what about the grocery store?"

"Right there. Trader Joe's is there, Vons is there."

"So you walk?"

"I walk. I mostly walk."

"Do you carry the bags?"

"If it's a one bag situation, I use my canvas bag with a shoulder strap. If I've got a huge amount, then I take the electric car. So walking is number one, biking number two, public transportation's number three, the electric car's number four, number five is my wife Rachelle's Prius. That's my order of choice."

Think about that. His fifth choice is a Prius. For most people that's not even a first choice. This man is a saint. I try imagining myself walking down Ventura Boulevard with a canvas bag of groceries strapped over my shoulder. Inside are organic fruits and vegetables, spelt muffins, and goat yogurt. As I said, I *try* imagining it.

"And who rides the buses?" Now I'm imaging a bus filled with eco-supermen like Ed, all with canvas bags slung over their shoulders.

"You know, people with the least amount of money take public transportation, not because they're green, but because it's the lowest-cost way to get around. Getting on a bike, taking public transportation—talk about low-cost ways to alter your carbon footprint. There's nothing cheaper. People in China have been riding around on bikes for years, not because they're environmentalists, but because they're broke. It's the cheapest way to get around. The fuel is a bowl of rice, a slab of tofu."

Before we start talking about tofu—and I actually eat a lot

of tofu, seriously—I ask if Ed will come over and take a look at my house and tell me what he thinks needs to be done.

"Sure thing," he says. "What I recommend that you do, Jeff, is pick the low-hanging fruit first. I did the cheap and easy stuff first. Energy-efficient lightbulbs, energy-saving thermostat, weather stripping around the doors and windows. If you're not handy enough to do weather stripping, you hire somebody to come and do it."

I am certainly not handy. If it wouldn't take so long, I would tell you the story of when I tried to caulk and ended up with caulk in my mouth, and I called the poison control center, and they thought I said I had cock in my mouth. Well, I guess I just told you.

"You do the lighting, the weather stripping, maybe some insulation in your attic. Before you even think about things like solar hot water, or solar electric, you want to reduce your bill as much as possible. Before you talk about producing, you want to talk about conservation. I'll show you all the stuff that I've done since I got started in 1970. I was a struggling actor, so I did all this cheap stuff."

"Back then you did it?"

"Yeah. I bought my first electric car in 1970."

"And you've lived in this house since when?"

"Eighty-eight. And the reason I got away with it for years was because I was single. I had sixty-eight degrees in the winter, and seventy-eight degrees in the summer, and I was happy. But then I got married—even before we got married, when Rachelle moved in here—and that lifestyle was over. Blow-dryers, curling irons . . . it's over."

"I know. It's a big bowl of over."

"Anyway," Ed says, "the first thing you need to do to change your carbon footprint is get a full physical, like you do at your doctor's. It's something I do every year. You need to have a full physical on your home. You need to have them come in with an infrared camera, with a blower fan for the front door—just like a cough and tongue depressor at a full physical. Like a CAT scan kind of thing, an MRI."

See? Didn't I say this whole mission was about getting healthier?

"They come in," Ed goes on, "and they'll give a full energy assessment of your home, and then make you a list. Here's the low-hanging fruit, here's the medium-hanging fruit, here's the expensive stuff, like solar electric. . . . You get to pick. I'll take some of column A, a few of column B, and one of column C. You can mix and match, and do as much as you feel you like doing—basically, whatever your wife will agree to aesthetically, you want to do."

"Good luck to me."

My wife is pretending to be supportive of my efforts to make the house greener and lower the family's carbon footprint. She cares, but she doesn't care that much. I foresee significant marital friction.

Now Ed leads me to the backyard.

"Is this real, this grass?"

"No, this is fake grass."

"I was about to say, 'This looks fake.' I mean, it looks real, but you know . . ." Is it a compliment to tell someone that their grass looks fake? As in, it looks so perfect, it can't possibly be real. Or does it come off sounding like an insult? Like, yeah, I thought so—I can spot a rug of fake grass quicker than a toupee. Who knows? Ed is the only person with whom you have to worry about this.

"Is that fake doody?" I almost just stepped in a pile of crap.

"The grass is so real, my dog's butt believes it."

I can't top that one. I contemplate fake grass in my backyard.

"I have two dogs who need to run," I explain. I love my dogs; have I mentioned that? "You'll see when you come to my house. My house has a lot of area for them to run. My dogs destroy the grass anyway. They invented destroying it."

"The first thing I did when I moved in was, I took out the lawn. I put in all this drought-tolerant stuff. And in the midst of that, I had one fruit tree, that lemon tree there, then I put in tangerine, orange, fig, California native plants, toyon, ceanothus, all sorts of lavender, and sage. It's more energy efficient. I'm lowering my carbon footprint if I'm growing food on-site. Now let me show you the fence, too," Ed says, leading me over to a white picket fence. "You walked in, you probably touched it. It's not wood."

It looked like wood to me. "It's not?"

"It's recycled plastic. Recycled milk jugs. Our countertop is made out of recycled Coke bottles. Rather than shipping it to China, you keep the recycled stuff here and make something out of it that you can use here. The other good thing is, I never have to paint it again. It's white all the way through. And do you see that red barrel there? We are going to replace it, put it underground, because I know it's kind of unsightly, but we collect rainwater there. I just use it for watering the trees. It's not good for drinking. I'm going to do what they call a potable roof. I'm going to have a membrane put on the roof, and then you can collect the rainwater and use it for all kinds of stuff."

He's putting a membrane on his roof. I can't imagine telling my wife that.

"Honey, I'm going to put a membrane on the roof."

"What?"

Membrane is a word for scientists.

Like I said, I thought going green was going to be the easy part of this plan. At first I thought Ed's house looked completely normal. Now that I've seen more, I feel like I'm on the set of *Star Trek*.

After that, he shows me his "smart thermostat" and his solar panels and tells me about all the money he's saved taking his home into the third dimension. The whole thing is pretty dazzling, but the question is: Can I take on a project of this scale? Do I have the commitment? And what's my wife going to think? This isn't about doing some recycling and buying Seventh Generation products. This is a major domestic overhaul. And I'm wondering if you have to be more than a little obsessed to pull it off. Maybe if I weren't already a food lunatic, my family could handle me becoming a green lunatic. We'll see.

5

I'm going to start today because it's Thanksgiving. Which is a really good day to start, because it has so much meaning with food, and just being flat out gluttonous. Almost everyone breaks their diet on Thanksgiving. I'm going to do the opposite. I'm starting mine. And then Friday, Saturday, Sunday, will be like my detox. I'll be home, and any anxiety I'm feeling in terms of eating correctly and changing everything will happen that weekend. Because Monday, the first of December, I start filming *Curb Your Enthusiasm*. So that will be, that *has* to be the official start. It has to be. No choice, okay?

All right, let's go. First, the stats. For these measurements, I'll be using the Wii Fit. BMI: 39.34. Weight: 298 pounds. Wii Fit age—that's right, Wii Fit age—56. According to a video game, I'm fifty-six years old. Dear God. I immediately ride for forty-five minutes on my Schwinn Airdyne. I must get younger.

We go to our friends' house for Thanksgiving dinner. And know that all day long, I am completely healthy. Believe me, I prepared for what I was about to do. Our friends serve the food buffet style. I go through all the different foods that I think are healthy. To see what is good, I put a little tiny bit of each choice on my plate. I sit down at the table with my family, our friends, their kids, and I'm eating all the little things off my plate. Well, all my wife sees is that I've eaten everything off my plate and I'm getting up for more. So she says, "Why are you getting more?" I start to explain myself to her, but then I begin resenting having to explain myself to her and being embarrassed in front of everyone that I'm explaining this to her. It was wrong of her, don't you think? So I say calmly, "I think I'm going to leave."

"Why?"

"I'm not feeling too hot."

"What's wrong?"

"Don't worry about it."

We drove separately; you know, with the kids, we sometimes come from different places.

So I get home, I'm really hungry, and I don't know what to eat, so I open our fridge, and I find half a Subway turkey sub. So on Thanksgiving I eat half a turkey sub, and I go to bed at about six o'clock. But what's amazing—and this never happens—is that I wake up the next morning, and there's a note on the side of my bed from my wife, apologizing. What a nice thing for her to do. Maybe it will be a nice weekend after all.

FRIDAY, NOVEMBER 28, 2008

Breakfast: goat yogurt, three Clementines, half of a navel
orange.

Snack: salt-free soup, banana.

Lunch: large salad.

Afternoon snack: salt-free soup.

Dinner: brown rice, cauliflower.

Exercise: forty-five minutes on the Schwinn Airdyne and an
hour of Pilates.

My wife asks me to be sure to clean the dishes after I'm done
feeding my kids breakfast. Spending any extra time in the
kitchen is just horrifying when you don't want to be eating and
eating is a problem for you. I love to make my kids breakfast,
but I usually make larger portions so I can eat part of theirs. I
never noticed that until today. So I make them smaller portions, because I'm not going to eat their leftovers.

The problem with cleaning the dishes is, of course, that's
when I eat whatever extra food is left on their plates. Any extra food. Hey, it's my children, so it's not gross. I bet some of
you do it, too, right? If there's a quarter of a sandwich left, I'm
going to eat it. This morning they leave quite a bit on their
plates. Pancakes and eggs. I don't touch it.

Today marks the first day of my detox. I've decided to
pretty much stay home so as not to have to deal with any
temptations. Luckily, I have the Academy screener of *Burn After Reading* to watch with my wife. But then watching it, when
the characters are in restaurants, I feel like I want to be in a
restaurant. I don't even like going out to eat all that much. But

watching this movie, I couldn't get enough restaurant action. Weird.

Tonight I'm all wired, and I can't go to sleep. I'm rolling in bed like someone coming off heroin. Look at me. I made it through the day sober.

SATURDAY, NOVEMBER 29, 2008

Breakfast: goat yogurt and shredded wheat, a banana.

Snack: salt-free soup and a pear.

Lunch: salad.

Afternoon snack: salt-free soup.

Exercise: twenty minutes on the Airdyne, twenty minutes on the elliptical, and forty-five minutes of weights.

I'll tell you about dinner later.

I start my day with Ed Coleman, who is my ninety-year-old golf teacher. I take lessons with him on Saturday mornings, and I have lunch with him at the Farmers Market quite frequently. He likes to eat there every day.

I like to be around older people, especially older people who know who they really are. There's nothing more enjoyable. Well, of course, there are more enjoyable things than an old person who knows who they are, but I like spending time with Ed—he makes me really happy. Anyhow, he tells me a story about when he was in his twenties and he himself was playing golf with an older gentleman. At a certain point the older man told Ed, "You've got a good swing."

"Thanks," Ed replied. "You know, I wanted to be a professional golfer, but I've suffered some injuries that have set me back quite a bit. So I guess it's not going to happen"

Then Ed asked the older gentleman how long he had been playing golf.

"Fifty-two years," he said.

Ed couldn't fathom that someone had done anything for fifty-two years. As of now, Ed Coleman, my teacher, has spent seventy-four years playing golf. It reminds me of when young comics ask me how long I've been doing stand-up. When I say twenty-six years, they can't believe it. I can't believe it myself because it's gone by so fast. It takes ten years before you really have an idea of what you're doing. But I can tell you that I'm still learning. I'm no comedy master. I think I'm pretty fearless, one of the better improvisers, and probably the most comfortable comedian in the business. That wasn't exactly what I was striving for, but I'll take it. Comfortable is good.

After golf, I work out with my trainer Anne. There are two other trainers at my gym, twins named Max and Mark; you can tell them apart because Mark has a birthmark on his face. They are forty-nine years old and they're in amazing shape. If you met them, you would think that they were thirty-five or thirty-six years old. They start telling me this story, my second unsolicited story of the day. Around twenty-five years ago, they were training at a park in San Diego, doing sprints. They were working very hard, when this man approached them and asked if he could work out with them. He joined them and kept up with their very rigorous workout. Afterward, they found out that he was fifty-two years old. They couldn't believe that he'd kept up with their pace. And now at forty-nine, they have never forgotten it, and it's a moment that truly inspires them.

It's good to hear stories like these because it's so easy for me to get depressed about my age. In my business, where ageism runs rampant, you are constantly battling to stay relevant. In order for me to do the work I need to do to be relevant, I need to be healthy first.

Now, dinner. One of the trials of losing weight is going out to dinner. The salt alone could kill you. I told my wife that during this book project we wouldn't be going out to dinner. She stared at me. She clearly wants her cake and to eat it, too. She wants a healthy husband, but there is sacrifice involved. Well, I couldn't have asked for a more perfect dinner than tonight's to get what I wanted, which is not to go out again.

We go out to an Italian place with two other couples. And shortly after our appetizers, one of the wives sitting across from me notices a red substance under her plate. My wife notices a red substance under her plate. Not on their plates, but under. I say, "Wipe it with a napkin, let me see it." So they wipe it, and I state, "That's blood." Not that I'm an expert on blood, but I know flat out, this is blood. One of the couples knows the owner, so I ask them to point him out to me, and then I walk over to him.

"Excuse me," I say. "This is kind of awkward, but we found some blood on the table. Take a look, it's here on the napkin."

He looks at the napkin, and before he can even say anything, one of his workers who's standing nearby says, "It's my blood, from my finger."

Now once one of your employees says it's their blood, you've lost. There's no arguing. What does the owner do? He says—to the guy with the bloody finger, mind you—"Get these people fresh napkins!" No exaggeration. Fresh napkins.

I sit down, and my table asks, "What did he say?"

"We'll be getting fresh napkins momentarily," I tell them.

Then my wife actually has to get up and say, "Could we get some disinfectant, and someone to wipe the table?"

Obviously, the rest of our meal is disgusting, everybody's stomach is turned, and we are waiting to see if the owner is going to do anything on the check. They should be giving us free meals there forever, not that I'd ever go back. The waiter (who, by the way, looks like a devil-worshipping magician with black-polished fingernails) comes by before bringing the check and says, "Can we do anything else?"

"No, we're good."

"No coffee, no dessert?"

"No, no, we're fine, we're fine."

Moments later he comes out with three desserts. There are six of us; he comes out with three desserts.

"This is for you. We hope that this will make up for the earlier mistake." Three desserts for six people makes up for a bloody table. Yes, the check comes, and no further effort is made to apologize. I think back to my mother, who, if she were in this situation, would go up to the owner, and start yelling at him, saying how dare he and that she's never going to eat there ever again. As a kid, I used to be horrified when she'd confront someone. Now I think I'd rather enjoy it. "You served me food covered in blood!" I can hear her saying. "Everyone should know!"

Obviously, I don't eat any of the dessert.

SUNDAY, NOVEMBER 30, 2008

There will be no exercising today, because I have no energy whatsoever. For breakfast, I have a small bowl of oat cereal of some sort, with rice milk and a banana. And then rice pasta for lunch and more rice pasta for dinner. I lie on the couch and watch football all day.

My wife asked me earlier if I thought our son Duke, who is eight years old, should sign up for baseball. I felt immense guilt, because I realized that the reason he doesn't know much about baseball is because I have not gotten out there and played with him enough. Today I just don't have the energy to do it. I feel terrible about this.

When I was a kid in suburban Chicago, I just went outside and all the kids in the neighborhood were playing baseball, football, and hide-and-go-seek, or whatever. But we live up in the hills. There are no kids in the street. You have to make play dates for them to play sports. Or I have to teach them. Fat dad on the couch.

My wife told me a while back, and she said it again today, that there's a "coach" who comes to your house and teaches your kids how to play different sports. I don't want anyone else teaching my eight-year-old son how to play baseball. I need to do that.

One summer I had plantar fasciitis; it's an irritation on the bottom of your feet. When it flares up, my heels really hurt and I have a great deal of trouble walking. That summer I had to sit down all the time. That was the first time my wife said to me, "You know, you can hire a coach to work with the kids." For a father, hiring a coach to play with your kids is the most demeaning thing you can think of. I imagine myself sitting in a chair with a blanket over me, like a ninety-year-old, watching as another man throws a football with my children. I said to my wife, "Why don't we hire someone to do the things for me that you don't do?"

"What do you mean?"

"All I'm saying is that's like me hiring a hooker."

She got the message.

As I lie in bed that night, I wonder, "Do I really want to be sober? Do I really want to lose the weight? Hopefully, to-morrow I'll get a bolt of energy, because as my body detoxes, I have no energy. The dieting and exercising are making me a little crazy. I still can't sleep and my wife isn't in bed yet, so I turn on the radio. The Elvis Costello/Burt Bacharach song "God Give Me Strength" is playing. It's about a love affair, but for me, I feel like: God give me strength; I don't know if I can pull this off.

6

Before we start filming the new season of *Curb*, our seventh, there's a story I want to tell you about how the show got started and how it coincided with a surprise crossroads in my life. It was 1998 and I was writing with Alan Zweibel, a very smart and funny guy who wrote for the original *Saturday Night Live* and co-created *It's Garry Shandling's Show*. He and I were writing a pilot for a show called *The Jeff Garlin Program* that HBO was producing for CBS. It was to be a companion show for *Everybody Loves Raymond*. They were actually developing two shows at the time for that slot, mine, and a show called *The King of Queens*. I think you know which show they picked.

Anyway, I was working at Alan's office in a little suite that he shared with Larry David and Billy Crystal. Billy was mostly out of town. Larry was in the office pretty much every day. I would walk around and take little breaks from writing (did I mention that I have ADD?). I knew Larry from our days doing stand-up, and sometimes I'd stop by his office and he would be singing Shirley Temple songs. Believe it or not, I knew them all. Our kids watched the same video of her songs. So he would sing and I'd join in. It went like this:

Larry: "Come along and follow me, to the bottom of the sea. We'll join in the jamboree—"

Both of us: "At the Codfish Ball!"

He would also come into Alan's office and talk to us when he got bored—that's what writers do, even when they don't have an attention disorder. You need to get up and walk around a little bit or else you go crazy. It's a good distraction, you know, to go bother other writers. And if they're busy, they give you the go-away-I'm-busy wave; you nod at them and set off to find someone else to bother.

Larry invited us to lunch one day and Alan couldn't make it, so I went. Larry hadn't done stand-up in a while because he had been producing *Seinfeld,* so he was asking me about the current scene. At that point I had developed Jon Stewart's and Denis Leary's HBO specials. And I always thought it'd be really funny to do an HBO special that was the making of an HBO special, a behind the scenes kind of thing without shooting the actual special. I described the idea to Larry and he loved it. That night he called me and said he wanted to do it. HBO had been after him to do something for a while. A few days later Larry, his agent, Ari Emanuel, and I pitched it to Chris Albrecht, the head of HBO at the time. I'll never forget Chris's reaction: "How can we *not* do this?" Which is exactly what you want to hear when you pitch something.

Then, on the first day of shooting, I remember Larry saying, "Wouldn't it be great to do this as a series?" From the moment Larry and I started working together, it was like we had been working together for twenty years.

After I was done filming the *Curb Your Enthusiasm* special, I had my last meeting at CBS to talk about my pilot, during which they told me they weren't going forward with my show. I felt pretty bad about it; I really liked the show and we'd put a lot of effort into it. Driving home from the meeting, I was heading north on Crescent Heights, and just as I was passing the intersection of Beverly Boulevard, the car in front of me suddenly stopped to make a left turn, and the car behind me rear-ended me. There wasn't great damage done to my car, but my neck snapped on impact, and it hurt. The pain wasn't outrageous, so I got out of the car, and the guy gave me his information. Looking back on it, I really feel that the guy was drunk. I should have called the police, but I didn't. I wasn't thinking clearly.

The next morning I woke up with the most extreme pain in my back and the back of my shoulders. The pain was so extreme that I went for a period of almost forty-eight hours without sleep, crying constantly in agony. My wife was pregnant with my younger child and, unfortunately, my mother-in-law was visiting us. I say "unfortunately" only because she still wasn't sure what to make of me at the time. In the past couple years I had just started to . . . well, earn a living. Prior to that, my wife was working as a casting director and I was a stay-at-home dad, taking care of our older son. I just got the feeling that until I was successful she wouldn't be too thrilled with me. It wasn't as if she were giving me the evil eye. It was something more akin to *I have my eye on you, big fella.* And the last thing you want is to be in a period of great vulnerability with some-one watching you.

I made a sincere attempt at putting on a brave face. But my back pain was extraordinary. At first I tried some acupunc-ture and massage. Then I finally went to a back specialist. He took X-rays that concerned him, and he said that I needed back surgery. I agreed to do it.

I remember, the night before the surgery, questioning whether I should go through with it. But I didn't feel like I could call the hospital the night before and say that I was call-ing it off. We were too far along.

Despite my reservations, the surgery was successful. By the way, the thing I hate most in the world, other than nausea and Nazis, is waking up after surgery. It's so unsettling and so shock-ing. I've only had surgery once, but I can't imagine that com-ing out of it is ever a joy. Except for the fact that you know you're alive.

The recovery seemed to be going fine, but my wife started to notice that my left eye was drooping. At this point she was not doing well emotionally. Who could blame her? She was pregnant with another child, and her husband was gimping around with a droopy eye like the hunchback of Notre Dame. I figured my eye would get better as soon as I recovered from the surgery.

One morning, about three weeks after the operation, I woke up and the room was kind of spinning. I thought I might have an inner ear infection, so I called the doctor, and he called in a prescription for antivertigo medication. But I was rapidly feeling worse—the room was still spinning, I was a little bit nauseous, and it seemed like the TV was floating over me. Marla called again and told me the doctors wanted me to come to the hospital immediately. I went, and they told me I was having a stroke. I was too out of it to truly understand what they were telling me. It must have hit my pregnant wife like a ton of bricks.

The doctor wasn't going to tell me that the stroke was brought on by the back surgery, although it had to be. Also, I was heavy. But I was only thirty-six years old. Thirty-six years old and heavy: you're not supposed to have a stroke. My parents flew in. But I didn't let them stay in the hospital that much. I'd rather they helped Marla.

I could barely walk and I spoke with a pronounced slur. What kind of life would this be for Marla? What an embarrassment for my children. Would I be able to participate in the rest of their lives? I also thought that I was never going to act again, never do stand-up again, that my career was pretty much over—just as things were really falling into place. *Curb* was going to become a TV series. We were due to start casting in a couple weeks. I was convinced that my days as a performer were over.

After you have a stroke, you're extraordinarily tired. When I say you're tired, I mean, you have to sit down after walking from one room to another—you're that exhausted. Recovery from a stroke, if you're lucky enough to recover, is not gradual. You feel awful for a great deal of time, and then one morning you wake up and you're somewhat better. It's a couple of months of nothing, and then suddenly there's a jump. You pray that this will keep happening.

I still have some balance issues—not with walking or standing, more with minor things, like going on a roller coaster. Which is actually fine by me. I have never liked roller coasters. Come to think of it, they've always made me nauseous. Maybe these balance issues really have nothing to do with my stroke; perhaps I just have an aversion to roller coasters. So how about that! I am fully recovered from my stroke.

At that point my doctor discovered that I had diabetes. He told me that diabetes can be brought on by great stress, combined with being in poor physical condition. So if you're planning on getting in a car accident that leads to back surgery and a stroke, I suggest getting in shape beforehand. You never know.

As we went into casting for the first season of *Curb Your Enthusiasm*, I couldn't quite walk yet, so I used a golf club instead of a cane to help me hobble along. (It's funnier to walk with the help of a golf club.) And by the time we started filming, I still wasn't really better. If you watch the first season now, I am so strokey. I didn't let anyone know how tired I was. Filming a TV show is very tiring if you're fit, let alone recovering from a stroke. But *Curb* was the best rehab I could have had. Just the improv alone did wonders.

I'm so lucky to be involved with a television show like this. I'm crazy lucky. It's one of two things I always tell my children. Be lucky. Be lucky and take what you do seriously—just don't take yourself seriously. I work very hard at everything I do. I take everything I do very seriously. I just don't take myself so seriously.

My biggest problem with recovery was that I wasn't taking my health problems seriously. I was still eating poorly, maybe more poorly than ever. I put on a ton of weight after the stroke; I eventually got up to 320 pounds. Not an accomplishment to be proud of.

What saved me from certain death was the Pritikin Longevity Center in Florida. It's a wonderful place that teaches you about health, nutrition, and exercise. They advocate a primarily vegetarian, low salt, low fat, and no sugar diet. It's kind of like summer camp for adults, except everyone is obsessed with food and disease. I first learned about Pritikin from my wife's aunt and uncle, who suggested I go immediately. I did, and it saved me. I'm going again as soon as we are done filming for the year.

7

MONDAY, DECEMBER 1, 2008
Weight: 298 pounds
Blood Sugar: 178
Exercise: 45 minutes of cardio, 30-minute swim

Today's reading from my book of meditations is about emotional distress and eating—turning stress and anxiety into
hunger, and how that hunger can never be satisfied. All true,
but I'm quite cynical as to whether or not I can handle my
"distress" as I film *Curb Your Enthusiasm* and write this book.
Maybe the meditations will help. I'm going to read one every
morning.

We start filming today at Larry David's house in Brentwood. Larry David's character's house, that is. We're filming
scenes with a doctor and the Black family. I'm not in any of
the scenes, which will be good for me in terms of focusing on
eating well.

I can't believe we're starting our seventh season of *Curb*.

We call it *Curb*. It's easier. You can call it what you want. I
don't care. Go ahead, I'm not kidding. Call it *Grandma's Cock*
if you so choose. As long as you watch it, I don't care what you
call it. I'm very proud of *Curb*.

My new assistant (she started today) just knocked on my
trailer to tell me it's lunchtime. I am absolutely not going to
fire this assistant. Not only am I determined to change my reputation, but this girl used to work for my wife. So I must try to
make it work. Her job is to keep me filled with fresh fruit and
vegetables; this is her primary responsibility. If she can handle
that one task, we should get along just fine.

xxxxxxxxxxxxxxxxxxxxxxxxxxxxxxxxxxxxxxxxxxxxxxxxxxxxx
xxxxxxxxxxxxxxxxxxxxxxxxxxxxxxxxxxxxxxxxxxxxxxxxxxxxx
xxxxxxxxxxxxxxxxxxxxxxxxxxxxxxxxxxxxxxxxxxxxxxxxxxxxx

I go to lunch and have some lovely macaroni and cheese
(growing up, my mother referred to food as "lovely"—"I made
you a lovely tuna salad sandwich, enjoy!") and a piece of cake,
actually, two pieces. So instead of coming back here and finishing what I was writing, I go to sleep. I get very tired after
eating poorly.

I should never go to the craft service table. I said to one of
the production assistants, if you see me too much at the craft
service table, I want you to punch me. Don't even let me know
it's coming. Just hit me in the head." He laughed. I hope he
doesn't listen. He wouldn't. But I'm sure I've made a terrible
mistake by telling him to pay attention.

Guilt makes me overeat. That's today's meditation. I have to say that, yes, I overeat because of guilt. I've overeaten because I'm sad. I've also overeaten because of happiness. I've overeaten because the wind blew in a different direction.

No cardio today. I overdid it yesterday. Also, I'm not going to weigh myself or take my blood sugar for a while. Maybe I'll only do it once every two weeks. I'm going to be in denial for a little while. Actually, I can be in denial on the blood sugar thing. But as far as the weight goes, I guess I'll just try avoiding mirrors.

I don't like looking at myself. I would say at least half the work I've done in film and television, I've never seen. Maybe three-quarters. (Maybe that's why I've seen *WALL-E* so many times.) I have to watch *Curb* because I'm a producer, and I have to watch the cuts early on. But if I go to a restaurant and there's a mirror, there is no way that I'm going to sit facing the mirror. I cannot. I am not comfortable with eating and watching myself. I don't care if it's a salad or an olive, it doesn't matter. I cannot watch myself.

xxxxxxxxxxxxxxxxxxxxxxxxxxxxxxxxxxxxxxxxxxxxxxxxxxxx
xxxxxxxxxxxxxxxxxxxxxxxxxxxxxxxxxxxxxxxxxxxxxxxxxxxx
xxxxxxxxxxxxxxxxxxxxxxxxxxxxxxxxxxxxxxxxxxxxxxxxxxxx

I just had some pizza. Some pizza and a nap. The character of Leon (played by JB Smoove) is eating pizza in the scene that we are filming today. I didn't intend on having pizza, but as I'm watching the scene, our prop master, Dort Clark, asks me if I want any.

"No thanks."

"You sure? Because I bought a ton of it."

"No."

"It's good."

"Okay, I'll have some."

Some was three pieces. Now I feel guilty *because* I overate. Oh well, I'll start fresh tomorrow.

WEDNESDAY, DECEMBER 3, 2008

Exercise: 45 minutes of cardio

My meditation says that *compulsive overeating is not a sane way to live*. Therefore, I am insane.

We are filming in Brentwood at Bob Einstein's character Marty Funkhouser's house. I'm excited because we're filming with Catherine O'Hara today, and she's one of my comedy heroes. I'm a little nervous because my character is supposed to have sex with her character—off camera, but I'm nervous just the same.

I just wandered over to the craft service table to calm my nerves and discovered this yogurt, granola, and fruit concoction. It's crazy delicious. Delicious and loaded with sugar. As I'm eating it, people are coming over and saying, "Good for you for eating that." That's how fucked up my eating has been. They congratulate me on devouring this sugary treat. After two bowls I'm done and ready for my sex scene. I've decided that yogurt will be my official pre-sex-scene food. It's light yet filling. However, no granola because that gets in your teeth. Then again, my scene is off camera. . . .

THURSDAY, DECEMBER 4, 2008
Exercise: 45 minutes of cardio
My meditation today is about how *belief in a higher power will get you the food you need.* I have no idea what this means.

We're filming in Brentwood again. It's a scene where Larry runs into Cheryl (Cheryl Hines) and Wanda (Wanda Sykes) at a restaurant. I was hoping my new assistant would get me the food I need. And I hate to say it, but I'm starting to realize that she is not really on top of things. She's supposed to check with the caterer before lunch to make sure the food I want is there. Today the caterer doesn't have any food for me. So I eat the same food as everybody else. I probably eat more food than everybody else. None of it is healthy. But to my credit, we are shooting in an area of Brentwood with a bunch of little food places. I have plenty of chances to buy food that is bad for me, and I don't do it. Got to give myself credit where credit is due. Also, notice the amount of cardio I'm doing.

FRIDAY, DECEMBER 5, 2008
When I'm overeating I don't accept any challenges except overeating. The thing is, overeating is not a challenge. It is a way of life—one that is easy. Not challenging. If I were in a hot-dog

eating contest, then that would be a challenge to see how much food I could shove into my stomach. But normally overeating does not amount to a challenge for me.

I'm not in any of the scenes today. I should be using this time to write or exercise or do both—now, that's a real challenge. In my opinion, sometimes we shoot too much. Way too many takes. It's not brain surgery. So having the ADD and not being in the scenes today, I'm bored. I find myself walking to the craft service area and eating a great deal of yogurt with granola. I'm eating it four or five times a day. Things are not going as well as planned, even with the cardio.

SATURDAY, DECEMBER 6, 2008

Tonight I take my son James to see AC/DC. He loves them. I was able to acquire backstage passes. When we get to the show, we are shown backstage. I always feel uncomfortable in these situations. Either I'm the only person with any degree of fame and I'm being stared at, or I'm the least famous person by a mile and I wonder what I'm doing there. I actually do my best to avoid the backstage festival. However, it's not about me—I am doing this for James. I would do anything for my boys. Actually, there is a lot I have already done. For instance, when he was younger I took James to all the Pokémon and Digimon movies. I'd fall asleep and James would wake me up to tell me I was missing the good part. I'd pretend I was happy he did.

At first my son and I are the only ones backstage. It's quiet. I tell him, "See, the backstage isn't so exciting." Just then a few other people are ushered into our area. It's Eddie Van Halen, a woman, and Eddie's son, Wolfgang. No one says anything and we all just stand there. I'm trying not to look at them. My son, of course, is staring. I look up, and Wolfgang is looking at me. No one is saying anything. A few minutes later someone comes out and ushers them into AC/DC's dressing room. And once again my son and I are alone in the large hallway.

"How about that?"

"Yeah."

"Let's get going."

"Okay."

We make our way up the stairs to a VIP area. It's rather crowded. There are plenty of drinks and food. The only thing I can eat, especially because I'm in front of my son, is fruit. I've already eaten dinner, so it's not that big of a deal. Or so I think. My son excuses himself to the restroom and I immediately make my way to the table where they have mini cheeseburgers. I suck down as many as I can before he returns. As I am wiping the evidence off of my mouth with a napkin, an old acquaintance of mine walks up to me. ("Acquaintance" is a word I like, even if spell check has to correct me every time I type it. Everyone out here claims to be a "friend" of anyone they know. But there's a difference between an acquaintance and a friend.)

So this acquaintance approaches me. It's Jon Faverau. I've known Jon since my Second City and Annoyance Theatre days. He's gone on to be a big success. The thing that impresses me the most is how fit he is. In our Chicago days, we were both heavy. I still am. No more cheeseburgers for me tonight.

MONDAY, DECEMBER 8, 2008

My meditation explains that *compulsive overeaters are always thinking about food—wondering if we are getting enough or too much, or if we're eating the right kind of food, and if we'll be hungry tomorrow.* Me, I never wonder if I'm getting enough food. I always get enough food. More than enough. But I know I'm always eating the wrong food, and I know I'll be hungry tomorrow.

Meanwhile, word has spread amongst different crewmembers that I'm writing a book. So any time I walk near the craft service table, I'm watched. And there's another problem: my assistant is constantly asking me if I want any "soupy." I eat salt-free soup as a snack.

"Do you want some soupy?" That's apparently the nickname she and her boyfriend have for soup, and now she's referring to it as soupy with me. The first time she said it, my response was, "Soupy?"

"Yeah, soupy."

"Dear God."

"What?"

"You've got to do me a favor. Please. I'm begging you: never call it 'soupy' again. At least not around me." That would be a new one, even for me, firing someone for saying "soupy." I would be a legend.

TUESDAY, DECEMBER 9, 2008

Today's meditation is about how *abstinence is the key to developing our potential.* Actually, this is true. If I'm not abstinent, then

I can't fully function as a person. This is the only thing I've read in this book so far that I don't think is a little bit goofy.

We are filming at my character's house in the Pacific Palisades. In this scene, I have a dinner party with Larry, the Funkhousers, Catherine O'Hara's character, Dr. Ball, and his lover. I'm eating a salad. Dort asked me what I wanted in my salad because I have to eat it over and over and over again. I probably should have just eaten the lettuce, but I have them put black olives in it. I eat at least one hundred black olives. As an actor, you have to eat a lot on-screen—at least that has been my experience. Maybe this has something to do with the characters I play.

When I was first getting started, I didn't know the various ways to deal with eating scenes. You may not know that I was in *RoboCop 3*. I played the donut jerk. It was early on in my career, and I didn't know what a spit bucket was. Maybe you don't know what a spit bucket is. A spit bucket, or spit bag, is a bag that you either have nearby or that somebody brings you during an eating scene, and you spit the food out. Needless to say, the guy that carries around the spit bag does not have the best job in the world.

Anyway, my character in the donut shop was always eating donuts, and so, during a twelve-hour shoot, I'd eat donut after donut, sometimes up to thirty-five donuts. At first I was excited. I thought, *Wow, I get to eat all these donuts*. (I also did a McDonald's commercial years ago for Egg McMuffins without a spit bag. But I only ended up having twelve or so. Let me tell you, I've done both, and if you have the choice, you want twelve McMuffins over thirty-five donuts.)

Anyhow, we filmed all night. No spit bucket for me. I ate these donuts all night long and I felt like I was going to puke by the time I got back to the hotel. It was like I had the flu. I felt horrible. Then the actor who played the bad guy in the scene—a good guy in real life—said, "Go to your room. I'll be there in two minutes." He came to my room, laid out some bright green marijuana, and said, "It's sinsemilla. I'm going to roll this. You're going to smoke it for like a minute or two, and then you'll feel better."

"I don't smoke pot."

"Trust me."

I was so nauseous that the only peer pressure it took to get me to try it was *trust me*.

I smoked it for a few seconds and I don't remember anything except waking up twelve hours later, and then we went out for fried chicken and I felt great. I literally don't even remember falling asleep. I slept in my clothes—I've never done that. Best fried chicken I've ever had. Smoking pot equals lots of fried chicken. Not a hobby I should take up.

WEDNESDAY, DECEMBER 10, 2008

Take things one day at a time. If we look too far ahead, then we lose our confidence. I think about what this one means. It seems important.

We are filming at a restaurant in Santa Monica. Today's scene is the one where I tell Larry that Richard Lewis got a blow job from his girlfriend on the way to the restaurant, and then Larry doesn't want to kiss her or take a sip from her drink. Luckily, we don't really get to the eating part of the meal, we just drink water.

I have devised what I think is a great system today. I walk out the back of the restaurant and around to the side of the building where the craft service area is set up. I grab a bagel and cream cheese and gobble it down before walking back on set through the front door. I do this all day. I feel bloated for the first time in quite a while. The sad thing is I'm not hungry; I do it out of habit.

At least the other thing I do out of habit, almost obsessively, is recycle. No matter whether or not I am overeating, I always manage to recycle what I can. I've been recycling for more than thirty years. That may sound like an exaggeration, but when I moved to Plantation, Florida, at the age of twelve, there was already recycling then. At first it was just for newspapers, but shortly thereafter, they started recycling plastic and glass, too. I remember listening to Marvin Gaye's "Mercy Mercy Me (The Ecology)" as a kid. I loved that song, and it really marks the first time I became aware of pollution. From the moment the concept of recycling was introduced to me, I loved the idea that just by separating my trash, I was saving trees, rivers, beaches, and just generally not polluting.

The show recycles plastic, foil, glass, and paper. But it's up to you to do it. The problem is that a lot of people on the show aren't doing it. At first I would look into the garbage can and if I saw recyclables, I'd move them to their proper places. (Now, I suppose I have to admit that I've taken things out of the garbage for other reasons, reasons I'm not proud of. For instance, I once threw out a box of Pop-Tarts, and a few minutes after I threw them out, I changed my mind. I really wanted one more. So about fifteen minutes later I went over to the garbage, fished out the foil-wrapped Pop-Tart, and ate it. I can't say that had anything to do with retrieving recyclables from the trash.) These days I'm going up to people in the cast or crew and offering to dispose of their plastic food and drink containers. For instance, I'll be in Larry's trailer and will point to the plastic dish that contains the remnants of his lunch, and say, "Are you done with that?"

"Yeah, why?"

"Let me take it. I'll recycle it."

"It's not even rinsed yet."

"That's all right, I'll do it."

"Go ahead."

Then I take the container to my trailer, rinse it out, and put in a drawer. When my drawers are filled with recycling, I take the stuff home and recycle it myself. I've gotten to the point where I don't trust anyone else to recycle. A new paranoia for a new age.

The interesting thing is that recycling is all about habits. I don't even have to think twice about it; it's second nature to me. But I have years of practice behind me. With eating, I have years of bad habits to overcome. Forming good habits is hard work. Sometimes it's hard not to be cynical. We are a nation of fat polluters. I am no poster boy for health and wellness, but at least I'm fighting the fight.

If this book of meditations is right about abstinence being

the key to success, maybe it's right about taking everything one day at a time. I'm going to give it a try. Tomorrow—no bagels. I'm sorry. Today—no more bagels. I'll worry about tomorrow later. I mean, tomorrow.

THURSDAY, DECEMBER 11, 2008

My meditation tells me I should *learn to set realistic goals* . . . I wouldn't have accomplished anything in life if I had "realistic goals." Actually, I wonder if *no bagels today* is realistic.

We are filming in a doctor's office in Santa Monica. Our trailers are parked on the beach, so today my office is under the warm sun. Maybe it's the beach or maybe I'm just more focused on making today count, but I have a great day with my food. And, yes, I know I haven't exercised for eight days.

FRIDAY, DECEMBER 12, 2008

Abstain from overeating one meal at a time. Whatever. Haven't we already been through this?

I don't have to be at work until later in the day. We are filming a scene where Larry discovers me with my pants down in my car after I've driven it off the road. When I arrive, I have already eaten dinner and I am done eating for the day. Or so I thought. There's still another meal on offer because we are filming so late. So I have a second dinner, and I have more from the craft service table. Now I'm bloated and angry. Not a good way to go into the weekend.

MONDAY, DECEMBER 15, 2008

Today's meditation is about how *we are sick with a disease*. I guess I am sick, but I know that most of the world does not look at compulsive overeating as a disease. They look at it as behavior easily overcome through diet and willpower. Everyone thinks it's simply a matter of diet and willpower. I wish it were.

Today's the final day of shooting until next year. I feel like too many people are watching my every move, so I walk off and have lunch at the Brentwood Country Mart. I eat some macaroni and cheese. And a cookie.

This has to stop. Thank God in a few days I am off to the Pritikin Longevity Center. I can't wait.

8

I'm standing with a full-figured gal outside of the rental car office. I've just taken a much-delayed flight from Los Angeles to Miami. I'm drenched in sweat and I'm hungry. The rental car finally arrives and the trunk won't open. The young lady with me is the manager. She apologizes and requests another car for me. Again, we wait a long time. She asks me why I'm in town. I tell her that I'm going to a place called the Pritikin Longevity Center to get healthy. She asks, "Is it a rehab place for drugs and alcohol?"

"Actually, it's a rehab for people who eat too much pizza."

"Rehab for fat people?"

"Yeah, but not only for fat people; it's for anyone who's lived unhealthily as far as food or exercise are concerned."

"I could use a place like that."

"Pretty much everybody could."

"I really need to lose weight."

She really does, but I don't say that. Instead, I say, "Maybe a little, but you can do it." I'm so full of shit. She needs to lose a ton. However, she is pretty. I wonder if she was ever thin.

She says, "You're nice, but I need to lose a lot more than a little."

"I'm telling you, you can do it."

"Really?"

Here I go: "I'll tell you the secret. You have to get so focused that no one and nothing can stop you. You have to be like a crazed animal. I'm telling you, *no one* can stop you. Plan your meals and follow through. Eat healthy foods. Exercise. Exercise like a maniac. Do an hour of cardio every day. Take up Pilates, weights, yoga, and tennis. Just keep moving. I'm telling you, you're a crazed animal. You cannot be stopped. And before you know it, you'll look and feel the way you want. Forget the way you'll look. Which will be beautiful, I might add. You're very pretty. You should enjoy that. But the way you feel—that's the reason to do it. You'll feel amazing."

"I don't know what to say. This is very inspiring."

"Believe me, you can do it."

"I'm going to do it!" she declares.

At this point, you realize, of course, she is taking advice from a hungry fat man.

My car finally pulls up. Except it's not a car; it's a huge SUV. She tells me that they'll give me the SUV for the same price as the car as an apology for the problems with the first one and the long wait. I thank her and tell her that I prefer a car. She informs me that actually all they have are full-size vans or SUVs. Oh well, so much for reducing both my footprints at once.

As I load up the SUV with my luggage, she thanks me for the advice. "I'm really going to do it," she tells me. "I'm going to get crazy focused and do it. I can't thank you enough."

Knowingly, I say "My pleasure." As I drive off, I yell out the window, "You can do it!"

I then head immediately to Lester's Diner in Fort Lauderdale and order a Trucker's Omelette with hash browns and suck it all down with a chocolate milk.

Normally, I go to Pritikin for a week; this time I'm staying for three. The center has exercise classes, exams with physicians, crazy healthy meals, and health education classes. When you get there, they weigh you, measure your body, take your blood pressure, and do complete blood work so they can see all of your numbers. When I first went to Pritikin in 2003, I weighed 320 pounds and I had huge numbers. Numbers like . . . well, let's see, what counts as high cholesterol, 230? They stop measuring cholesterol at 1,000. Mine was over 1,000. Literally off the charts. So if I tell you that Pritikin saved my life, I would not be lying.

Pritikin attracts different types of people, mostly from the U.S., but also from all over the world. They are mostly middle-aged, some older, some younger, some fat, and a few very healthy people (the ones who keep coming back). When you first arrive, they give you a badge to wear around your neck. On the badge are stickers indicating how good or bad your joints are, whether you have high blood pressure, diabetes, a bad back, etc. You see people with badges that are completely covered with stickers. My first year was a sticker festival. My badge looked like a piece of lost luggage that had made it around the world without me, a rainbow of bad health. Your goal is to not have any stickers. I won't wear a badge anymore. They can't make me.

A nurse from the medical department calls my room and wakes me up at 6:30 a.m. This nurse does not only wake me in the morning; if I ever take a nap, she somehow figures it out and she calls. You can put a "do not disturb" hold on your phone that stops all phone calls except the ones from the medical department. This morning she's calling to remind me to come by for my blood test. They test your blood constantly here. They want to document how their program changes your numbers. I tell her I'll be right up.

Before I go up to medical, I test my blood sugar. You want your blood sugars to be below 120, ideally below 100. Mine on day one is 174—lower than I expected. They want your blood sugars first thing in the morning and late in the afternoon. I bring my own testing kit, because if you have it done at the medical office, it's almost as if they get joy out of hurting you when they prick your finger.

The nurses, as a whole, are lovely. There are special nurses who take your blood for elaborate testing, and I always try to get this older Latina nurse. She is quite good. Not a lot of poking. And with all my health problems, I've been poked and bruised more than a hooker on heroin. Anyway, the lovely Latina nurse is not there, and I get a guy who has ripped my arm to shreds before—like a hooker on heroin. As he pokes me with the needle, I prepare for the worst, but I get lucky and am off to breakfast with a Band-Aid on the first try.

In the dining room I meet up with my friend Jessica (real name). I met Jessica at an earlier expedition to Pritikin. She wants me to use her real name in this book but doesn't want me to say exactly how much weight she's lost. I'll say that when I met her she was big, and now, not nearly as big. She is truly an inspiration, and a great pal. She and I like to go to Pritikin at the same time.

Every morning Jessica gets us our *New York Times* and *New York Post*. We don't do a great deal of talking in the morning, mostly just reading and eating. She always saves us a booth. There is no assigned seating at meals, thank God. You can sit in a booth, which seats four at the most, or you can sit at a table that can seat eight. The tables are a bit risky. After the first day you start to realize who is nuts and who is not. It's a roll of the dice as to whether you sit with someone who is wonderful and extraordinary, or someone who is going to drive you insane.

Once, at the breakfast table, I met an amazing guy who was involved with building the bullet train that Obama talks about, a train that would cross the country in about ten hours, powered by magnets. You either meet people like that or you meet the most entitled, negative, complaining, rich cocksuckers. That's an opinion, by the way. You rich cocksuckers can't sue me for that. Some people can't complain enough about the food, though most of them change their tune after a few days.

Let me explain the food at Pritikin. It's low fat, no salt, no sugar, and primarily vegetarian. Once your body gets used to the lack of salt and sugar, your taste buds come alive. The food (created by Chef Anthony—more about him later) is amazing. Since I've gone to Pritikin, my taste buds have changed so much that all the salt that restaurants add to food repulses me. When I go out to dinner, I have to remember to ask the waiter to make sure that there is no added salt or I'm screwed.

Also, when I go to Pritikin, I eat only what I'm supposed to eat. I don't take extra. And whenever you see people taking extra all week long, or not liking what's served and asking for something to replace it, they are always the people who complain that they haven't lost any weight at the end of the week. Sometimes people bring their own salt. (I've even had servers offer me salt, as if it's contraband and I'm in prison.) I've seen people bring their own wine. People bring bread. There are people who have fast food delivered to them, in their rooms. One time I heard about a doctor getting in an elevator with a patient, who had just come back from the grocery store, carrying a bag filled with a bunch of crap. And when the doctor asked him about it, he said it wasn't his—that it was in the elevator when he got in—and left the bag of groceries behind when he got off on his floor. It's amazing to me that people would pay good money and just ignore the program. When I go, I follow everything to a T. You name it—exercise, workshops, eating—I follow the rules exactly. It's easy. It's all controlled for you. When people complain about not losing weight, I ask if they followed the program exactly. They always say no.

Breakfast is my favorite meal. I generally have a bowl of

oatmeal supreme (oatmeal made with soy milk and served with bananas, apples, and raisins). I also peruse the fruit buffet. Usually I have a big bowl of blueberries, blackberries, watermelon, and pineapple, a glass of water, and a cup of tea. They also have egg-white omelets made with fresh vegetables, if you choose. I rarely do, because I'm usually too full. As soon as I finish, I'm off to exercise.

Every morning there are exercise classes in different time slots. The classes are named after local sports teams—there are the Dolphins, the Heat, the Panthers, the Hurricanes, and the Marlins (I know that marlin is plural, talk to the team). I don't know if there is rhyme or reason as to what class they assign you. But you find all ages and all levels of fitness—some people are in their late eighties and recovering from life-altering surgeries, and some people are in their twenties and quite physically fit. Most people are somewhere in between.

In the cardio classes there is every type of equipment, from treadmills to ellipticals to machines where you just exercise by sitting down and pedaling with your arms. Yes, your arms. Music plays with a constant thump that seems to exist to remove my will to live. A trainer leads you through the classes, telling you to go faster, then slower, then faster, and occasionally stopping to help you take your pulse.

Having been to Pritikin five times before, I do this all my way. It's not as selfish as it sounds. I arrive whenever I want and pick an empty machine. Hopefully, it's an arc trainer, which is like an elliptical, only a little more difficult. I bring my iPod and headphones, which blocks out the thumping and the trainers. I like listening to music from NFL films—

it's orchestral and very inspiring to me. Actually, the music reminds me of watching football in the seventies, which then
makes me wonder how in the hell I ever got here. The music
also has some sound bites mixed in. My favorite is a coach telling his team, "You can get it done. You can get it done. Once
more, you've got to get it done."

I never look at the TV monitors in the mornings because
they're always tuned to the news channels. And believe me,
when you are trying to change your life, the last thing you
need are talking heads feeding you a bunch of crap without
any of the facts, or watching constant footage of a tsunami or
a fire. Once I was on the elliptical, and I am not kidding
you, a monitor was tuned to the Food Channel. They were
making a pie. I swear.

This morning, however, the disturbing vision is not on the
monitor, it's right in front of me. A few years back, possibly the
first time I came to Pritikin, I was in a group with an enor-
mously fat couple who looked like they were in their late forties. They turned out to be one of the great Pritikin success
stories. They each lost more than a hundred pounds and have
kept it off for at least five years.

Well, this morning, the woman, now in her fifties, is exercising across from me. Clearly, having lost all the weight has
given her a better sense of self. Actually, it's given her an inflated sense of self. A hugely inflated sense of self. She is wearing a half-shirt and the smallest pair of shorts I've ever seen.
The only person who should wear something like this is a
Sports Illustrated swimsuit model. A new one. Not even Cindy

Crawford, who is still ridiculously beautiful, could pull this look off. It's jaw-droppingly wrong. It's a big bowl of wrong. Please make it go away. I want to leave. But I'm on a mission. Suddenly, watching the news doesn't seem so bad. So I pedal away for forty-five minutes. As soon as I'm done, I report my accomplishments to a trainer, who then takes my pulse and records it in my file.

The cardio is followed by weights or by stretching and abdominal exercise sessions. I usually eat some fruit and then lift weights with my favorite trainer, Terri. I love her like a hooker on heroin. I promise that's the last time. Here is a little lesson in comedy. If I keep repeating that hooker reference it would stop being funny; however, it would get very funny again after another twenty or so mentions. I mean, really funny. I don't want to do that to you. But just know that I could. Terri works me crazy hard, but she's quite empathetic. She never pushes me further than I can go, but sometimes further than I think I can go. I have to say, in that area, it's fun to be proven wrong.

Next, I grab a couple of apples and head back to my room, where I take a shower and collapse on my bed. I doze off and the phone rings. It's that nurse I told you about, calling to remind me that I have an appointment with my doctor, Dr. Bauer, Thursday afternoon at 4:15. I tell her I'll be there, hang up, and fall back asleep. Minutes later the phone rings. It's her again, "Make it four o'clock, not four fifteen." I grumble okay, and leave the phone off the hook as I drift off to sleep.

The first few days are always difficult. As your body gets used to eating right, you become quite lethargic. This lasts for a couple of days. Finally, on the third day, you feel so different. That's actually an understatement. You feel great and have so much energy that it's like there is a rocket up your ass. I know a rocket up your ass doesn't sound so wonderful. But it's a special ass rocket that's comfortable and gives you lots of energy.

I wake up just in time for the first lecture of the day. The lectures are usually about nutrition or medicine. They are an hour long and, boy, are they great. Yes, great. Some border on amazing. Yes, the food is great at Pritikin. And the exercise is great. But believe it or not, the lectures are the thing that stays with you long after you leave. I've learned so much about reading labels, calorie density, the metabolic syndrome, and the diseases of affluence, that I'm no longer funny. See, right here would've been a good spot to keep the hooker references going.

Often in these lectures run by the Pritikin doctors and nutritionists, you hear the most incredibly stupid questions. For example, during a lecture on calorie density, after the lecturer states that oil is high in fat and not good for you, someone will ask if it's still okay to use it. And the lecturer will reply, "That's your decision, but know that it's not good for you."

"But I really like it."

"It's up to you. I just gave you the facts."

"Gosh, I just love it. What about in salads?"

At this point the nutritionist will try to move on.

They also offer a cooking class. Chef Anthony usually teaches them. About halfway through the lecture, all these fat people come in because they know that at the end of the class, they're going to be serving food. The most popular ones are the dessert lectures.

After the lecture I'm joined at lunch by my friends, Jessica (once again, real name) and Zeke (fake name of his choosing). I also meet up with Zeke (fake name of his choosing) every time I come to Pritikin. We sit at a booth with our gigantic salads, served in bowls that are bigger than my head. But this is not your typical salad. There is no cheese or tuna, and the dressings are all ultra low-fat with no sugar or salt added. Not a fun salad. It's a salad that fucking means business. It's a salad that says, "I'm gonna fiber your ass up." The idea is to fill up on your salad so that you won't want an entrée. Lunch is my least favorite meal.

Jessica (real name) and Zeke (fake name of his choosing—you get it, I'll stop) notice a couple across the room. The woman is much younger and very attractive. Zeke decides that they are Israeli spies. When the lady gets her food and moves around the room, Jessica notices that she's staring at me.

"Bullshit."

"Look at her," she says.

I casually look her way.

"Oh my God!"

"Told you."

"It's so blatant."

Zeke is still convinced that they are Israeli spies.

I immediately leave and go to my room.

About an hour later I go out to the pool and participate in some water aerobics. It's mostly old ladies in the class. Pritikin is located at the Turnberry Isle Yacht Club, so the people in

the condo share the pool. Every year that I've been here, I've
seen the Tanning Family from Philadelphia. Tanning isn't
their name, it's what they do. It's all they do. Every day, all day,
they lie by the pool: the father, the mother, and their two
grown sons. After a couple of days they look like they're star-
ring in a minstrel show.

The water aerobics are led by the clinical director of exercise, Ivan, who is a handsome Cuban man with a thick accent.
He's very serious. When he counts off, you hear the full enun-
ciation of every word. "O-ne! (beat) T-w-o! (beat) Th-ree
(beat)!" I'm bouncing around in the pool with a bunch of old
ladies and I can barely keep up. Afterward, I'm exhausted.

The afternoon snack is salt-free soup. There are no noodles in
the soup. Not a fun soup. There's fruit, too, but I can't have
any at this time of the day because of my diabetes. After two
cups of soup, I feel better. But I'm still extremely tired. I need
to lie down. I skip the second lecture and go back to my room
and collapse on my bed. It's a good nap. Of course, the phone
rings. Yes, it's that same nurse. She wants to again remind me
that my next appointment is still on Thursday, but at 3:30. I
fall back asleep until the phone rings again. And yes, it's her
again.

"Why don't you come at four instead?"

"Okay."

"Don't forget."

"You won't let me."

"You're very funny."

"Please stop calling."

She giggles and hangs up.

Dinner is the only meal at Pritikin that's not served buffet style. Sometimes at dinner you'll see these old men, sitting alone at these group tables, looking very lonely. And then, come Friday night, they're at a table with a very young lady in a pretty dress; needless to say, these are hookers. They'll have a hooker there, eating steamed broccoli.

Unfortunately, there are no hookers tonight. What we do have is salad, more salt-free soup, and a piece of salmon with a bunch of vegetables. Once again, I'm sitting with Jessica and Zeke. Joining us is a know-it-all girl from St. Louis, an older lady who is obsessed with *Curb Your Enthusiasm*, and a couple from Georgia, who I'm sure has never dined with a real live Jew before. Here is a snippet of our conversation. For fun, I'll let you figure out who's talking.

"I hear that you're some sort of celebrity."

"Me?"

"Yes, we heard . . ."

"He's on the best show on television."

"What show is that?"

"It's called *Curb Your Enthusiasm*."

"Where would we find this show?"

"It's on HBO."

"We don't get HBO. Too much nudie stuff."

"I don't own a television."

"I don't watch television."

"I don't like this soup."

"I don't either."

"Really? I think it's delicious."

"Will they make me a veggie burger?"

"I'm sure they will."

"I asked them for cheese on my vegetables and they said yes."

"Really?"

"I'm kidding."

"What is this show of yours about?"

"It's not my show. It's Larry David's show and I'm just lucky to be involved."

"Who's Larry David?"

"He created *Seinfeld*."

"We never watched that show."

"I haven't watched TV for six years and counting. And to be honest, I don't miss it."

"Good for you."

"Yes."

"Do you read?"

"Only the classics."

"I like Bradshaw Wagner. Is he a classic?"

"I don't know who he is."

"I really don't like this soup."

"Are you going to the gym after dinner?"

"Definitely. Are you?"

"Yes, after the lecture."

"Great. I'll go after the lecture, too."

"Oh, waiter! Would you take this soup away?"

"Oh look, it's the spies. And she's staring at you."

"Spies?"

"Of course, from other spas."

Tomorrow night, a booth.

I go to the lecture after dinner. Due to my ADD, even the littlest thing breaks my concentration.

Tonight, it is a man whose cell phone rings during the lecture. You'd think he'd turn off the ringer or maybe take it outside. Nope, he answers it.

"Hello? Franco, how are you? Yes. Yes. I heard."

Then he says to all of us, "Excuse me." And he heads out of the room.

Jessica, Zeke, and I roar with laughter. No one else does. Clearly, we're getting punchy. Even though this lecture is interesting, I can't control myself and I start to behave poorly. Every time the nutritionist who's giving the lecture makes a point, he pauses and smiles before moving on. I lean over to Zeke and ask him to imagine the lecturer filling each of these pauses by pulling out his penis and slapping it on the podium. With every pause and smile, out comes the penis. Zeke draws a picture of the penis on the podium. This is fun.

Next, Zeke and I head over to the gym. We both do another half hour of cardio. There is no one else in the gym. We watch *The Andy Griffith Show* as we gallop on.

At the end of the day Zeke and I sit by the pool and talk for a while. We both laugh about the fact that he's chosen the name Zeke. Sometimes it really does feel like camp here.

I go off to bed knowing that tomorrow will be pretty much the same. Only three more weeks.

In addition to training with Terri, I work with a trainer named Tom. He works with individuals like Zeke and me, but he's best known for his Thursday night lecture, called "Posture For Success." Tom is rumored to be near eighty years old, and he's a rock of a man. Quite imposing. Dare I say, strapping. When you first start working with Tom, he gives you a sheet of mantras. A few examples:

> You are in your body 24/7. Be aware! Be proud! Be the best you can be all day, every day.
>
> You can leave the gym, but you never leave your house (your body). Stop taking it for granted. You need it! It needs you.
>
> You are here. You've paid the price of admission; great facility, great possibilities. The rest is up to you. What are you willing to do? You must make the difference. You CAN make a difference, but you have got to do it for YOU.

Trust me, he is one of the great characters of all time. My first session with him is in one of the studios at Pritikin that are mostly used for yoga and Pilates. They have hardwood floors and the walls are mirrored. First, Tom takes my measurements—and then comes the humiliating part. I take off my shirt, and he comes over and pulls my pants up about six inches above my belly button. Then he tells (maybe even yells at) me to pull my stomach in, hold up my chin, and he tells me to hold up my chin by saying "kiss." He wants me to look in the mirror with my chest in and to kiss. To see myself standing there, with my stomach sucked in and my shorts pulled up to my chest is the single most horrifying visual I've ever witnessed. Worse, for instance, than a community theater production of *Pippin* or *The Pajama Game* (I can't remember) that a girlfriend is in and you have to go or she'll break up with you. But at the party after the play she breaks up with you anyway because she prefers a guy in her cast that wears leg warmers. More horrifying than that.

The next evening I attend a diabetes seminar. The lecturer says that the American Diabetes Association issued a statement in 2005 warning that in twenty years diabetes could be the largest epidemic humanity has ever faced. By 2025 they predict 300 million cases of diabetes worldwide. In 1980, there were fewer than 30 million cases. Underdeveloped countries have no diabetes, due to a minimum of processed food and a lot of daily physical activity. My eyes dart involuntarily over to a lady drinking Gatorade. Meanwhile, when I get up from my seat, Jessica says I look like the evolution of man—the first few steps I'm hunched over, and shortly thereafter, I'm standing tall.

Another lecture I attend is about becoming your own Pritikin chef. Chef L. Anthony Stewart is from Jamaica, therefore, he's fun to listen to. I don't know how to write in a Jamaican accent, so you'll have to add the accent yourself.

"Pritikin's task is to get rid of irresponsibility, permissiveness, and carefree attitude. Do simple things that you are capable of maintaining."

"Plan what you're going to eat."

"Grill, steam, broil, bake."

"No salt, oil, butter, or margarine."

"Don't assume that your food is healthy. The culinary arts is all about the fat, cream, and salt."

A woman comes in forty-five minutes late and asks, "What kind of pots can we cook in?"

Here are some things I hear at other lectures:

The kidney is not designed for as much salt as we are eating.

Disease of affluence leads to: obesity, hypertension, diabetes, heart disease, stroke, common cancers, Alzheimer's disease.

Your blood pressure goes up with higher dietary salt intake.

Most cancers are self-inflicting.

Your body wants more calories when it eats calorie-dense foods.

I bet you didn't think you were going to learn anything in my book, did you?

The next morning I'm feeling a little sick of the gym, so I decide to walk outside. There is a beautiful path around a golf course. As I'm walking at a nice quick pace, I think I'm being passed by everybody. This includes a guy walking backward, a pregnant woman, and an old lady wearing flip-flops.

Now, get this. That afternoon I'm finishing up a swim and as I'm about to leave the pool, I notice the Israeli spy on a deck chair. In a bikini! (You don't see a lot of bikinis at Pritikin.) With a camera! Staring at me! I have my doctor's appointment in fifteen minutes. What do I do? I stay in the pool and try to think of something. I wonder if her superior is standing by, ready for the memory card hand-off. But why would Israeli spies be interested in me?

Then it occurs to me that they're not Israeli spies. Maybe she's planning to sell the picture to a tabloid. But what tabloid would care? What would the headline be? JEFF GARLIN IS ACTUALLY FAT AND WE HAVE THE PICTURE TO PROVE IT. After about ten minutes of waiting her out, I get out of the pool right in front of her chair and stare right back at her. And you know what happens? She says hello and offers me a towel. I take the towel and walk off to my doctor's appointment.

You cannot eat anything between lunch and 4:00 p.m., because they need to test your blood sugar again. They prick my finger to get a drop of blood on a little plastic strip that's attached to a small meter. My number goes down to 115. I'm pleased. I'm also a little bit shaky. I need my afternoon snack.

Before I can go, they call me in to see my doctor. He's one of the original Pritikin doctors; he's been there for, I believe, twenty-seven years. I should probably fact-check that . . . then again, I'm not a journalist, and I did say, "I believe." He's in, I believe, his eighties. He's also a character. He's always asking

me about my groupies. I explain that I don't have any groupies. He smiles and winks at me and says, "Whatever you say."
He's pleased that my blood sugar has gone down, but says that
it shouldn't have been as high as 174 to begin with. He can't
say too much more because he doesn't have my lab results yet.
He gives me a speech about taking things seriously. Which obviously, I don't take seriously because I'm way too hungry and
can't think about anything other than my afternoon snack.

I'm going to tell you right now that what happens next is quite
embarrassing.

On the morning of December 31, 2008, I drop off Jessica
and her dog at a little dog park in Hollywood, Florida. I leave
to go pick up some diabetes medication. Know that at this
point, I've already lost about ten pounds at Pritikin and I feel
great.

At the pharmacy, they say my medication won't be ready
for half an hour. I have a half hour with nothing to do, and
I know that right up the road is Jimmie's Chocolates. Yes,
Jimmie's Chocolates, located off Federal Highway in Dania
Beach. I dream of Jimmie's Chocolates. Who buys chocolates
while they're waiting for diabetes medication? I guess I do—
the same guy who, in the past, has bought Twizzlers and Pop-
Tarts along with his Glucophage.

As you can imagine, Jimmie's Chocolates smells like
heaven. I'm greeted by a big, friendly woman with some sort of
accent.

"May I help you?"

"Um, yes. I, uh, want to pick out some chocolates."

"How many?"

"I don't know. How about one of those and one of those."

And then I choose one of those, and one of those, and one of those as well.

After she weighs them, she starts wrapping them in a gift box. Their assumption is that you're not buying all these chocolates for yourself, that they are a gift.

"I don't need a box. Put them in the bag, a bag's fine."

"It looks so much better for you to have a box."

Looks better to whom? To me and myself? I don't argue. She even puts a ribbon on the box.

I also buy a giant chocolate alligator with little candy eyes. It just looks like fun. As soon I get in the car, I vacuum down the different chocolates. Caramels, milk chocolates, orange cream . . . these are fucking great chocolates. But I'm feeling nothing. They don't do anything for me. I'm not jazzed, and I'm also not even wracked with guilt. There are no emotions involved. And I think, *Well, this doesn't do any good.* Because, really, the purpose is to shove down my feelings. But I'm in a good place; I'm just doing this out of habit.

I drive back to the Walgreens to pick up my prescription. But instead of going in, I sit in my rental car parked between Publix and Walgreens and eat the chocolate alligator. I eat the head with the candy eyes last. I will always remember exactly where I was when I ate chocolate for the last time. I go in and get my diabetes medication, come back to my car and throw away the box with all the wrappers, I mean, evidence.

As I drive back to pick up Jessica, I think about the term "compulsive overeater." It's not the overeating; it's what you eat. Nobody ever got fat because they couldn't stop eating apples.

I pick up Jessica and her little dog Briscoe (real name).

"I got my medication."

She finds the ribbon on the seat. "What's this?"

"That's the ribbon from a box of chocolates that I ate."

She laughs. I laugh back.

"Oh, I also had a big chocolate alligator. It was delicious."

She laughs even harder this time. "Right," she says.

I'm thrilled she doesn't believe me.

She'd be so sad and disappointed if she knew the truth.

She'll only find out when she reads this book.

About a week later I'm exercising in the gym alone one weekend morning. I have not slipped up since the chocolate incident; it didn't lead to more bingeing. I actually feel good knowing that I will always remember when and where I ate my last chocolates.

I'm on the elliptical watching *The Good, the Bad, and the Ugly*. I've seen it many times. I'm watching the scene where the good guy (Clint Eastwood) is making the ugly guy (Eli Wallach) dig a grave. The good guy says to him, "In this world, there are two kinds of people, my friend. Those with loaded guns and those who dig. You dig."

I begin to move faster.

• • •

At lunch Zeke and I are telling Jessica how impressed we are with her weight loss. She did it all the Pritikin way. It really is inspiring. Here's what she said to us: "It's really, really hard. But you can do it. But it's hard! It takes years."

No one ever talks about how hard it is. They just tell you that you can do it, or you should do it. No one ever says, "By the way, this is going to be hard." You would never go to a Weight Watchers meeting and hear them say, "Here, you eat your foods, you do this, you do that, and oh, by the way, this is going to be really, really hard. Good luck."

On the way to my final doctor's appointment, Tom sees me walking and yells at me to pull up my pants. "Be proud!" he tells me. I do feel proud. I've lost fourteen pounds and lowered my blood sugar to 101. But I don't pull up my pants.

9

When I get home from Pritikin, my wife tells me that, once again, her New Year's resolution is that I should lose some weight.

I say to her, "Do you know what you just said?"

"No, what?"

This tells you something about the extent to which my wife is involved in my health and weight issues. She loves me and really wants me to get healthy. I appreciate this and I love her like crazy. But her vigilance can lead to problems between us.

Once, it caused me to steal. Let me explain.

I'm shopping for dog food with my wife, and next to the pet store is a grocery store. She tells me, "I'll get the dog food. You go get some garbage bags and I'll meet you at the car." Great. Good plan. I go in the grocery store, and my blood sugar's feeling kind of low, actually, really low. I start to get shaky and weak. I'm in the produce section so I grab the first thing I see . . . well, to be honest, I don't grab the first thing I see, which is an apple. I could have. I could easily have gone to the organic apples. Instead, I get a Caramel Kit Kat. Which, by the way, if you enjoy caramel and you like the Kit Kat, they've done a wonderful job. It's fantastic. A lot of times these companies experiment, and it doesn't turn out so well. Inside-out Oreos come to mind. How about Strawberried Peanut Butter M&M's? The name alone. Caramel Kit Kat: home run. It's delicious.

Now I can't find the garbage bags. I can't find them and I'm running out of time. My wife comes in and my reaction is all wrong. I get scared and yell out. And, mind you, it isn't like she sneaked up on me—she was coming right at me! I shouldn't have eaten the Kit Kat. I've got the wrapper in my hand. She asks, in reference to my yelp, "What was that all about?"

"I was just daydreaming," I say. And she falls for it. Lucky break. But then she asks, "What's in your hand?"

"Why? What are you talking about?"

"What's in your hand?"

"Nothing."

"Something's in your hand."

"There's nothing in my hand." I put my hand in my coat pocket.

"What are you putting in your coat?"

"Nothing!"

"You're putting something in your coat. What are you putting in your coat?"

"Nothing!" I point down the aisle. "Maybe the garbage bags are over there. I didn't check over there." She looks away, giving me just enough time to turn, pull out the wrapper, put it in my pants, and turn around with my hand back in my jacket pocket. What a brilliant maneuver!

"What are you putting in your jacket?"

So now I can have fun. "What are you talking about? Nothing! Want to check? Go ahead! Go ahead!" She sticks her hand in my pocket and do you know what she pulls out? A Trident wrapper. How great is that? I'd left a Trident wrapper in my pocket. How perfect! So now I can play it up. "Hey! Is that where we're at? No sugarless gum? What's next? Water? No water?" So then we walk to the checkout line and I'm thinking, *Well, how am I going to pay for the Kit Kat? What am I going to do?* I say to her, "I'll pay for the garbage bags and then meet you out by the car?"

"No, I'm fine," she says.

I can't push it. Then I started imagining that when I pay for the bags, I'll pull a dollar out of my wallet and flip it at the guy. But then I also imagine him saying, "Sir, you just flipped a dollar at me. What's going on?" And my wife saying, "Why did you flip a dollar at him?"

So we walk to our car and I don't pay for the Kit Kat. The wrapper is in my pocket, and it's weighing on me. I'm really unsettled by the whole thing. We get in the car and drive off, and there's a sense of relief, but also a lot of anger, at myself. Yes! Anger! Because I have chosen the possibility of arrest over pissing off my wife. That's sad. My wife has got problems with food and me, or, more accurately, she's got big problems with my food problem. Of course, she only cares for me; she only wants me to live. Recently, she said something that really got to me.

She said, "If I'm going to the grocery store and I see a man in one of those electric carts because he's too heavy to shop, I think, 'Oh God, please. Please take care of yourself, Jeff.'"

MONDAY, JANUARY 12, 2009

Our location today is in the Palisades at the fictional Danson house. We're filming a scene where it's Ted and Mary's anniversary party. My daughter sings for them, poorly, and Larry stops her. After filming, Ted and Mary tell me about a new diet that they are following. Ted insists that I should eat a piece of avocado or chocolate with every meal. Imagine me telling people I gained all of the weight I lost at Pritikin by eating chocolate at every meal. When people find out you're on a special diet they always tell you about *their* crazy diet. Then again, Ted and Mary are both fit and good-looking.

By the way, the house that we're filming in has a screening room in the basement with all sorts of candy. Lot's of chocolate. I don't have any.

TUESDAY, JANUARY 13, 2009

Today's meditation is that overeating is hell, that a binge becomes torture. I think "torture" is too strong of a word. "Not pleasant" is a better term. Maybe "sad." But not "torture."

We are filming at the W Hotel in Westwood. Larry has to carry Denise (a woman he's dating who's in a wheelchair) up the stairs of the hotel to dinner. One of my great joys, which helps me take my thoughts off of food, is to fool friends and colleagues. Once, I paid a location scout twenty dollars to tell all the guest actors that he collects lotions from around the world. All innocent, stupid pranks. But I love it when they work. I used to make lots of phony phone calls before caller ID ruined everything. My favorite person to fool is my mother. Once I convinced her that I was a deliveryman with a soap delivery for her. It confused her. But I kept her on the phone for twenty minutes. Tonight I convince a crew member that I used to run the bar at the hotel and I'd sell honey to my customers. I tell her that the honey was so popular that people ordered it from around the world. She believes me, which I enjoy to no end. My producer and friend Erin makes me tell her the truth. She always does that. I'm telling you, if it wasn't for caller ID or Erin, I could do this all day and never gain a pound.

WEDNESDAY, JANUARY 14, 2009

My daily meditation is about how *we are willing to go to any lengths to stop eating compulsively*. It assumes we are willing, when it should actually say that if we are *serious*, then we should be willing. Truth be told, it's rare for a fat, compulsive overeater to hit bottom like an alcoholic or a drug addict. No one is ever about to lose their job because they ate too much at lunch. Nobody looks in his friend's eyes and can tell he's had too many cookies.

My kids have Cinnamon Toast Crunch for breakfast. I come back from Pritikin and I can hardly bear to look at this stuff.

And now I can read labels. I'll lay some of my Pritikin knowledge on you.

Here's the first lesson: whatever you read on the front of a box is a lie. The only thing you should really be eating is fruit and vegetables, but if you're eating out of a box, only go for the stuff that is the least processed. The less it's processed, the better. Common sense. All right, you know that. But the companies try to make everything look healthier than it is.

I have this box of Cinnamon Toast Crunch in front of me. I promise I'm not going to eat it. Just study it. It says, "Whole grain guaranteed in every box" in big, yellow letters. And they put the words "whole wheat" and "rice" in bigger type on the front. I don't know about you, but I know it's bullshit when they start enlarging the font size.

And then the box lists the calories, which are "enlarged to show details," in case you're an idiot. Only calories from fat matter. Calories don't mean shit. It's the calories from fat that you have to look out for, and you should never eat more than 20 percent of calories from fat. So each serving is 130 calories, and thirty of them are from fat. Is that too much fat? That is correct, ladies and gentlemen, it's only a little over the limit, but enough that it will make a difference.

Then you go down to sodium. Calories from fat and sodium are the only things you have to worry about, I swear to God. You should never have more sodium than there are calories. So there are 130 calories and 220 milligrams of sodium. That means: way too much salt. Believe it or not, there's enough salt in some celery sticks to fulfill your daily salt intake.

We don't need much salt. Now, mind you, if you're running twenty miles, you might need more salt.

The last thing to check on the label is the sugar content. The first ingredient listed is whole grain wheat, and the next is sugar. That means there's almost as much sugar as whole grain wheat. And they also add rice bran oil, which is sugary; fructose, in addition to the sugar and added color; and BHT to preserve freshness, which means you can keep it on the shelf for many years.

One small label contains all of that information once you know how to read it. I don't say any of this to my kids. They don't need the burden of this information now. They just need to learn to think about food normally, not obsessively. Believe me, I think about this all the time. How my being a compulsive overeater is probably hereditary. I think my biggest motivation to be fit and healthy is to show my boys that it can be done. Do as I do, not as I say.

Today we film a scene at Northridge Hospital, where Larry asks the doctor for his home phone number. Phillip Baker Hall is the doctor. No one breaks Larry up more in a scene than Phillip Baker Hall. Phillip never breaks, but Larry loses it. I'm lucky because it's a short day of filming. When I go home, in order not to eat, I go to sleep.

THURSDAY, JANUARY 15, 2009

My meditation today is *If we slip, we sometimes feel that since we haven't been perfect, we might as well go ahead and eat a lot.* That is so true for me. I always start the day perfect.

We're filming a scene in the Palisades where Larry is on a date with Denise (the girl in the wheelchair). I see someone eating cake and am overcome by the feeling that I need to get to an OA meeting. Just having been at Pritikin, I am aware of these things. I know I am vulnerable. Just then I see an acquaintance of mine, Stewart, who is a psychiatrist who specializes in addiction. Seeing him is like a sign, a sign that if I ask for help, I'll get it. As I talk with him, I begin to feel better and the urge goes away.

Remarkably, as I'm talking to him about my problems with food, he's eating an ice-cream cone. That's the thing about being a food addict as opposed to a drug addict: it's almost impossible to stay away from the source of your addiction.

SUNDAY, JANUARY 25, 2009
Weight: 273
Blood Sugar: 110
Wii Fit age: 47

I've decided that every two weeks I'm going to check my numbers. I don't want to obsess about them, so every two weeks sounds good. I'm not using the Wii Fit to exercise. Just for my weight and age. I'm still confused about how it knows what my age is based on me standing on some video-game platform. LOTION.

MONDAY, JANUARY 26, 2009

They say in OA if you fail to plan, then plan to fail. You're supposed to write down your meal plans. Truthfully, I've heard this before. This and write down everything you eat. I'm bored even writing about this. Notice that I stopped recording what I ate every day almost two months ago.

We're filming in Westwood at Matteo's restaurant. In this scene, Larry is mad at the Dansons for taking Susie and me to a restaurant with a gift certificate that he gave them for their anniversary. I spend five hours eating dinner. In the past I would have had the prop department give me plates of pasta. Food scenes are a great way to binge with justification. Today my plate is filled with cantaloupe.

I spend five hours having dinner with Ted Danson, his wife Mary Steenburgen, and Susie Essman. They're so fun and interesting that I never get bored. My assistant, however, does something that makes me crazy. When we shoot all day and go into the night, they usually serve pizza. They serve pizza and very fattening Italian food: pasta with thick sauces and cheese, and lasagna. And she didn't prepare. She doesn't even know where she's going to get me dinner. Being hungry, I get frustrated. My assistant's main job, the job *Curb Your Enthusiasm* pays her to do, is to supply me with food. I'm not making this up. Her job is to supply me with the right food, healthy food. I can't be trusted at craft service. I can't. So she comes up to me and says, "I found a good Japanese restaurant. They say that the food is great."

"Who told you the food is great?"

"They did. When I called them. They told me the food is great."

"The restaurant that you called told you that their food was great?"

"Yes."

Holy crap! I don't even know what to say. I hope I don't fire her. I walk away and head over to the Italian food, and just as I was going to say, "Fuck it," my wife and kids show up for an unannounced visit. They never visit. So my kids had delicious Italian food. I have a piece of fruit to hold me off. My assistant orders the sushi. It's great. I'm glad I didn't fire her. And as a bonus, I recognize one of the extras in the scene we're filming; she was a *Playboy* playmate a few years ago. I don't tell my kids about that. They don't need the burden of that information now.

TUESDAY, JANUARY 27, 2009

Today's meditation is about *having enough and no more*. They say *enough is a feast*. I get it. I was taught at Second City that less is more. With improvising, that means if you say and do what's needed in the scene, then that's more than enough. Do

more and you can ruin it. The same goes with food. Eat what
you need. Eat too much and the meal is ruined.

We're filming all night at the Staples Center. We film a scene
where Larry and I are at the Laker game and we don't like our
seats. It's actually quite fun. We have access to all the stadium
food. I don't eat the stadium food. I don't like stadium food,
but that's never stopped me from eating a ton of it. Instead, I
become obsessed with whether or not the Staples Center
recycles, and I can't find anyone who will give me a straight
answer.

WEDNESDAY, JANUARY 28, 2009
Today's meditation is, *When we overeat, there is no room left for
the spirit. We feel like taking a nap rather than working.* Hungry or
not, full or having overeaten, I'd rather nap than work.

We are filming at the wheelchair girl Denise's apartment. It's
the first day since Pritikin where I finally eat something I
shouldn't. It's an empanada, a fried pastry filled with beef or
chicken, and they have one with just spinach and cheese.
They look fried to me, and Charlie, the crafty guy, says, "No,
they're not fried."

"Really?"

"No, they're baked."

"I'll have one."

Have one I do. And another and another. I lose count.

Tonight a group of film students from Boston University studying here in L.A. are observing. I explain to them what we are filming, and I answer their questions. They ask me all sorts of questions. But they should have asked me this one: "You seem rather jolly. Did you just stuff down some feelings by eating a ton of baked empanadas?"

"Why, yes, I did."

"Are you going to let this mistake spiral out of control?"

"No, I'm not. I'll start fresh tomorrow. Hell, I'll start fresh now."

"Good for you."

"Thanks."

The student and I both stand quietly for a minute.

"Any more questions?"

"I'm good."

THURSDAY, JANUARY 29, 2009

Today's meditation is about being more committed to loving than we are to overeating. *Loving makes us strong.* I think if I had more sex as a teenager I wouldn't be so fat.

I lose my temper on the set today, because we film too much. Boy, the shit my co-workers took from me early on when I was eating correctly and grumpy about it. And now it starts all over again because of yesterday's empanadas. *Yesterday's Empanadas* is the new name of this book.

TUESDAY, FEBRUARY 3, 2009

Today's meditation tells me that *Food is not the only problem. It's not only food, it's our life that's a problem. Our ego gets in the way of our sobriety.* My problem is that I don't have an ego about it, but I'm still not humble enough.

We are filming in Santa Monica. Our trailers are once again by the ocean. We are filming in an Italian restaurant, where Ted Danson sends a dessert to Larry's table and Larry rejects it, and of course, they fight. An extra tells me I look fatter on TV. I guess that's a compliment.

Later, at home, I'm thinking about this idea that my life could be the problem. I decide to call my mother and ask her about my childhood eating habits. Was I always like this? How can I make sure my kids avoid my fate? This is a question that haunts me. My mother, of course, is thrilled that I call. She loves me. She's a Jewish mother.

"What were my eating habits like as a kid?" I ask her.

"You liked Ho Hos. You loved Ho Hos and Twinkies. And Hi-C, which I probably shouldn't have been giving you, because it made you kind of hyper. But I didn't know much about ADD or any of those things at the time. I think I usually made you healthy dinners, though. You ate just about everything. There wasn't anything you didn't like. You were always a good eater. I never really had to worry about you. You loved when I made grilled cheese. I used to make you a lot of grilled cheese sandwiches, macaroni and cheese, cheeseburgers. Cheeseburgers: really big. Spaghetti. You used to like steak. In those meat-eating days, I used to make a lot of steak. And roast. And brisket. You used to love brisket. And pancakes! Pancakes, jelly omelets."

As she's talking it's like I can see my childhood self getting fatter.

"I remember that every day when I came home for lunch, you made me a milk shake with whatever I ate. An Ovaltine milk shake, with vanilla ice cream and milk. Do you remember that?"

"I don't remember putting ice cream in it, but I did have Ovaltine in the house, yes."

"And also, I remember that for years you would cook dinner and then put the food on the table so we could just keep on taking the food."

"That's true."

"When did I start to gain weight as a child?"

"You weren't a heavy child."

"I know. When did I start gaining weight?"

"You started gaining weight in high school after you had that heart problem. When you had that heart problem and you couldn't play football anymore. You were burning up a lot of calories by playing football, and so I think that had a big impact on you with gaining weight."

When I was seventeen I was diagnosed with Wolff-Parkinson-White syndrome, or WPW, which means you have this bonus abnormal electrical pathway in the heart that leads to periods of a very fast heartbeat. It made my mom worry about me more. It caused a lot of fights between us. I had successful surgery at twenty-seven to correct the problem.

"But I remember being heavier than the other kids in seventh grade."

"Absolutely not. I have loads of pictures of you."

"I remember in eighth grade, I was one of the two heaviest kids in my class."

"Look at your bar mitzvah pictures. You were not heavy. You were just tall. You're big boned and you're tall. But you were never fat. Absolutely not. You were never chubby."

"I disagree. I was already fat before I had heart problems."

"Nope. Look at your bar mitzvah pictures."

"I looked a little chubby."

"You did not look chubby. You looked really, really nice."

If only we could always be seen through our mothers' eyes! "So, when did I really start to balloon up, when were you really concerned?"

"I think more when you were an adult. When you were working as a comedian."

"When I started eating late at night?"

"When you were living on your own. I think that I had some control over you when you were living at home, because after many years I realized that there were no Ho Hos or Twinkies or anything like that in the house."

"I remember, you did put me on diets. What was the diet place we went to with the cards?"

"I did? Was it a Weight Watchers place?"

"No, it was a different company."

"I did? I don't have any recollection. You mean to help you lose weight?"

"Yeah. Did I overeat as a kid?" I persist.

"Only when you got older."

"But when I was little, you didn't notice that I overate as a kid?"

"No, I don't think you overate."

"No, I did overeat."

"But you weren't heavy. You weren't a fat child. I just found a very funny picture of you when you were in high school. You looked adorable. You didn't look fat at all. In fact, you were very muscular and you looked great. I don't remember you ever, ever being a fat kid. You got fatter when you went to live on your own. At least when you were living at home, I had some control over it."

"No, I put on most of my weight the very first year I started doing stand-up. I put on like thirty pounds from eating late."

"Right. I said, 'When you started to be a comedian and were living on your own.' "

"I was still living at home!" It didn't happen on her watch. I give up. "But was there ever a time that I was abusing food or too heavy, and you wanted to say something but didn't?"

"When you started your comedy, it was just about that time that you started putting on weight. I would tell you, in a nice way. But you would get very upset with me, and I was tipping on my toes to talk to you about all those kinds of things or if I didn't like what you were doing. If I didn't like what you were wearing, I would say, 'Jeffrey, why are you wearing that?' One night you went to entertain at a comedy club, you put on those Zulu pants. Remember those pants that were popular?"

"I never had a pair." I didn't. I swear. "I had some pants

that had some wild prints. But you're thinking of those Zubaz pants and I never wore those. Those look ridiculous."

"Well, you had something with lots of print. You were going to entertain. I hated those pants on you. I thought they made you look heavier, and I said to you, 'Don't wear those pants,' and you ran out of the house. And I looked at Dad and said, 'I can't believe he went out looking like that.' Because one thing about you, you were always a very clean and neat person. That's the one thing you do to this day. You always look trim and neat."

"Thank you." Like I said, if only everyone could see me through my mother's eyes.

"Even on TV, you're totally spiffy. And by the way, I just want to interject one thing: Evelyn and Mitchell went on a trip to Europe and they were on the plane for hours, and there were ten episodes of *Curb Your Enthusiasm* that they watched all the way to Europe."

"Oh, that's so nice. Okay. Let me ask you a question: Do you think that I'm ever going to lose the weight?"

"I don't give up the chance. I worry about you all the time. I know that you watch yourself and I know that you exercise and that you take care of yourself to the best of what you think your ability is. But it's not enough. And I would like to see you slim down because I know how serious it is when I think of my father. He had diabetes and then he died of a heart problem. If you must know the truth, there isn't a day that goes by that I don't think about it."

"I'm sorry, Mom."

"Listen, I want to tell you another story. You were in the

fifth grade and the teacher told me that you were disturbing the class. And I said to her, 'Why is he disturbing the class? What did he do?' And she said to me, 'He's making everybody laugh.' And I kind of chuckled to myself. I was thinking to myself, if that teacher would only know, if she saw you today, that you've made your career out of it. And I was called to school many times."

"But were you ever called to school because of food or ecology?"

"Was I what?"

I'm teasing her now. She doesn't even know what my book is about, so I tell her.

"You never told me. You never ever, ever, ever told me anything about your book. You zipped your lips. You didn't tell me. So, you're telling me that you're going to be a thin person?"

Good question, Mom. If only I knew the answer.

10

Today's meditation is: *Don't relax, a binge can happen at any time. Be on your toes.* I never relax.

Today, we filmed at my character's house in the Pacific Palisades. I ask Larry to lie to Susie about the panties she found in my glove compartment. I have to say, it makes a world of difference, creatively, when I'm in a scene versus when I'm not. I feel like I contribute so much more when I'm in a scene. Not only as an actor, but as a director and a producer. When I'm on my game and engaged in what I'm doing, I feel no need to overeat.

SUNDAY FEBRUARY 8, 2009

Weight: 271

Sugar: 108

Wii Fit age: 48

My weight is going down. Fantastic. APPLE BROWN BETTY.

TUESDAY, FEBRUARY 17, 2009

Today is about forgiving ourselves. *After we binge, it's important to forgive ourselves in order to move on.* I don't really binge anymore. At least, I haven't for a while. In the past, there was nothing to forgive. I would binge, binge huge time, and feel nothing. I felt no guilt. Just sick.

We film at the Banana Republic on the Third Street Promenade in Santa Monica. Larry's trying on pants and the fire alarm goes off and he has to leave with the sensor still attached to his pants. It is a lovely day in Santa Monica and once again our trailers are at the beach.

I've been quite good about my eating. During breaks in filming, I go into the Barnes & Noble across the street. I spend about two hundred dollars on books. On my way out, I notice a sign: BUY ONE, GET ONE FREE on select titles of their DVDs and Blu-rays. I spend another hundred dollars on select titles. I'm eating less, but spending more.

I have a problem with buying things on autopilot. There is this book called the *The Power of Now*; it's a bestseller. Okay, you want to know my life? *The Power of Now.* I bought it twice. Having no idea I owned it. And I've never read it! And I never will! *Night* by Elié Wiesel. The book about the Holocaust. I bought three copies of *Night*! Three! In one year. How do you do that? How do you not know that you bought *Night* before?

WEDNESDAY, FEBRUARY 18, 2009

Today's meditation is about setting priorities. *As an overeater, you have to make abstinence the number one priority in your life.* This is one I wish I could follow.

We're shooting at my character's house in the Pacific Palisades again, another scene about the panties. Before I explain what happened today, I want you to know that I do not enjoy sarcasm. In fact, I'm leading the charge against sarcasm. Sarcasm is one of the easiest forms of humor, requiring no comedic talent whatsoever. All you have to do is say the opposite, with a tinge of sarcasm in your voice, and you're off to the races. You're not being clever or funny, you're being sarcastic. I never do sarcasm, and I don't enjoy when people do it to me. I've launched into this diatribe for a reason. Something happened today that I regret.

Today I'm shooting part of a scene where I'm looking out the window of my house waiting for Larry to arrive. I'm going to explain to him that he's being blamed for the woman's underwear that Susie found in my glove compartment. So after we finish the take, I walk back to the video village, where the director, producers, and other assorted crew sit. And Larry's sitting there, eating a Larabar. Larabars are protein bars, all natural, a little high in fat. The thing is, Larabars are not tasty enough to want more than one. They're filling, and you enjoy it while you're eating it, sort of.

I know this rule from my current world of nutrition: if something tastes good, it's bad for you. I'm not talking about a banana or an orange. But, in general, when food is prepared, if it's really good, there's some crap in there that's not good for you. Take a great vegetarian restaurant. Maybe you go there because you think it's healthy. Trust me, if the food is good, it's not good for you. Is it vegetarian? Sure! Is it full of crap? You bet it is! Trust me on this.

Anyhow, Larry is eating a Larabar. A group of people is sitting around, and I say to Larry, "What are you eating?"

"Uh, a Larabar."

"Where'd you get it?"

"Your assistant."

For emergencies, my assistant keeps a supply of Larabars. So she gave Larry a Larabar. I've got a bunch of them; I don't give a shit. But I said to him sarcastically, "I told her not to give one to anybody!"

"I only ate half."

"Good."

I walk away and think, *Did he think I was serious?* A little while later I walk up to Larry and ask, "Did you think I was serious?" Sarcasm from me is the last thing he'd expect.

"Yeah."

"Oh, fuck, man. I was kidding."

"What do you mean you were kidding?"

"Sarcasm."

"I thought you were serious."

"That's the problem with sarcasm."

If you never do sarcasm, people think that you're serious. I say to Larry, "Do me a favor, and tell me exactly what you thought when I said that."

"I thought you were a huge dick. And I thought, 'Oh, it's one of the chocolate coconut ones, it must be his favorite. It must have set him off. I won't even eat it.'"

Let it be known, I owe everything to Larry David. There you go. I wouldn't own a house, I'd have nothing . . . okay, I'm going overboard. I can't say I'd be completely unsuccessful, but certainly I wouldn't have the life I have now, without Larry David. I thank him constantly. I do.

When the Chicago Cubs had me sing "Take Me Out to the Ball Game" at Wrigley Field, I called Larry on his cell phone and thanked him. Would the Cubs have wanted me without *Curb Your Enthusiasm?* Would I have gotten *WALL-E* without *Curb Your Enthusiasm?* A hearty no. I met Andrew Stanton, the filmmaker of *WALL-E,* at the *Finding Nemo* premiere, a movie he also wrote and directed. The reason that we talked was that he was a *Curb Your Enthusiasm* fan. Do you follow me? I'm a lucky man. And I have Larry David to thank.

So do you think that I'd be okay with him having one of my protein bars? We all know I have a problem when it comes to food, but do you think maybe that would be all right? I'm so embarrassed.

"It wasn't the first time I've done sarcasm, but a rare occurrence," I say to Larry. "But I'll tell you what it was . . . it was now the last time. I won't ever do sarcasm again." And I mean it.

You know you don't ever do sarcasm with kids. This is another big rule. Don't ever do sarcasm with kids. They always think you're being serious. So, having kids, I don't do sarcasm. My point is, thank you, Larry David, and fuck sarcasm.

THURSDAY, FEBRUARY 19, 2009

Today's meditation is about responsibility. *We need to be responsible to ourselves because we cannot change anyone else.* This one is huge. On all levels, but especially with addiction. I have friends who are quite heavy and it's difficult watching them destroy themselves. I've invited one of them to Pritikin multiple times and he keeps on making excuses, so I stopped asking. I have to keep reminding myself that there is nothing I can do. It's hard enough to control myself.

Every now and then I try to set an example for other people. And I mean that in the sense that other people should look at me as an example of what they don't want to become. For instance, when we were filming the pilot/special of *Curb Your Enthusiasm*, we filmed in Westwood, where UCLA is. We were shooting an establishing shot of Larry and me walking into a restaurant. As we were walking, we went by a cookie place called Diddy Riese. Diddy Riese sells huge bags of cookies for two dollars. It's like the owner doesn't care. "I want everyone to have cookies. Cookies for everyone. Forget profit."

Sitting in front of this place was a kid, maybe about twenty years old. When we finished shooting, they were setting up the cameras inside the restaurant, so I decided to hang outside where it was cooler. The kid was still sitting there. He was wearing Birkenstocks, ripped jeans, ripped T-shirt, a little ski hat kind of thing—which in L.A., by the way, is unnecessary. So he said to me, "You want a cookie?" Yes, I wanted a cookie. But I wasn't going to have one. Why couldn't I just have said to him, "No, no thanks. I'm good." Instead, I thought, *He's a young guy. I'm going to teach him something.*

Now, as you know, no one in his twenties wants to hear what Mr. Forties or Fifties or Sixties thinks, unless they ask you. If they ask you, then great. If they don't, then shut the fuck up. But this particular evening I chose not to.

I said to him, "How old are you, man? Oh, twenty. Yeah, yeah. Go to UCLA? Live in the dorms? All right, let me tell you something. You know what? The cookies. You could eat a whole bag of cookies, go back in there, get another bag, come back out here, eat that whole bag. Yep. You could do the whole thing. You know what? You could get a third bag, go back to your dorm room, hang out in your dorm room, eat some cookies, watch *Full House*, smoke some pot, eat some more cookies, call your girlfriend over, have sex, watch some *Full House* a little bit more, smoke some cookies, eat some pot, have more sex, then kind of freak out that *Full House* is over because you're really high at this point. Your friend comes over and says, 'Do you want to play soccer?' So you play soccer in the middle of the night. You break your ankle. You limp back home. You say you'll take care of it tomorrow. Have more sex with your girlfriend. But you're on your back this time because you can't really stand since your ankle's all messed up. Smoke some more pot. Have some more cookies. Remember you have a test. A final in the morning. Cram all night long. Go take the test, having not slept, still kind of high. And come back here after your test and get another bag of cookies and eat all of them. You could do all that, and you'd be just fine. Listen to this: If I have one cookie, I die. I am the future. And in the future, there are no cookies. I am the future: take a look. Now is the time. Now is the time for cookies." Anyhow, he didn't let me finish. He said, "If you don't want a cookie, just say 'no thank you,'" and walked off.

So today we're shooting this scene where Larry buys lemonade from my neighbor's kid. He doesn't like the lemonade and he calls the kid names. Today the whole group goes to lunch at a restaurant in the Palisades: the producers, the guest cast, the whole group. We're having a pleasant time, sitting at the front table by the window. At some point a guy comes up and asks the people in our group whose backs are against the window to "Please move in. Please move in." With a serious sense of urgency.

"What's going on?" we ask. He slides by and he takes a sign that says A out of the window and puts up a sign that says C. Now, know that those signs in the window tell you that you've passed state health inspection cleanliness tests. A is the best, then B and C. This place went from A to C as we were sitting there, after we had already ordered. People are always telling me that something happened to them that would be a great premise for the show. Trust me, nobody has ever given me a good idea. But this lowering of the rating would actually be perfect. Let's see if Larry uses it.

FRIDAY, FEBRUARY 20, 2009

Today's meditation is about OA being a selfish program. Because *sobriety is something that we want more than anything else, we need this program.* I wonder if my problem is that I don't want it badly enough.

We're filming in Woodland Hills at some innocuous offices for a scene about some NBC execs trying to sell Larry on doing a *Seinfeld* reunion. I have a bad day. I mean a *bad* day. I'm grumpy, and I'm snapping at people. First up is a lovely production assistant named Karie. When I say lovely, I mean crazy sweet. Anyway, she is walking me from my trailer to the set. She leads me to an elevator that takes us up one flight. I snap at her: "Why didn't we just take the stairs?"

Next up is an actor playing one of the NBC executives. After a few takes, I let him know that I don't like what he's doing and that I think he's trying too hard to be funny. When I leave the set, our producer Erin O'Malley asks me what's wrong. I have no idea what she's talking about. She tells me that Karie is upset. I apologize to her right away. I don't make any excuses. I just say, "I'm terribly sorry for being rude to you." That's all. Because, boy, when you're a jerk, you can't make any excuses. You just have to step up and do it. You can't start in about your food issues. You have to take responsibility. When I get home, I call the actor who I was rude to today. He is surprised that I'm calling, but he happily accepts my apology.

Later that night Pixar has a dinner at a restaurant downtown in honor of *WALL-E* and the Academy Award nominations. Many courses. I feel much better. Two thoughts: One, if you are a bit grumpy, go to a restaurant and have many courses;

and two, if you want to stay abstinent, eat healthily at home and sit with your feelings.

SATURDAY, FEBRUARY 21, 2009

Tonight, I'm a presenter at the Visual Effects Society awards. They serve a lovely dinner. (Thanks, Mom.) Also, they put some sort of chocolate dessert in front of me. I push it away. They put another one down. I move that one aside. Once again, they set another one down. After I move this one, I set my head on the table to stop the festival of desserts.

After the event Andrew Stanton and I go to a party. A party where they are serving dinner. I shouldn't go, but I do. Andrew and I find ourselves sitting with Peter Gabriel, who cowrote and performed the song "Down to Earth" for WALL-E. And it's truly one of the best dinner conversations I've ever had in my life. Both Peter and Andrew are artistic geniuses, and we talk about many things. One of my favorite things that we talk about is how adversity brings success. I barely touch my food.

SUNDAY, FEBRUARY 22, 2009

Weight: 268
Blood Sugar: 111
Wii Fit age: 48

I feel great, but I'm still too old according to my Wii Fit. PURIM.

TUESDAY, FEBRUARY 24, 2009

We're shooting a scene in a fake NBC lobby at the Warner Center, where Larry runs into Cheryl, who's there for an audition. This is a satisfying day for me. It's a rare occasion that I am really satisfied with my work as an actor. Good work equals no eat.

Also, I'm inspired by an article I read in the *New York Times* about the low-hanging fruit you can tackle when making your home greener—a term Ed Begley used with me, too. It mentioned using clotheslines instead of machines to dry your clothes. I love this idea. Almost 8 percent of all electricity in the United States of America comes from clothes dryers. It's true. Eight percent. Not only that, but when you hang up stuff, it comes out way better. It's warm from the sun or, at least, I imagine the clothes to be warm and wonderful. It will cost me about fifty bucks to hang the clothesline. My plan is to put it away from the house, all the way across my yard. My house is hidden, so the neighbors can't complain about the Appalachia factor.

When I get home my wife is not so thrilled with the idea.

"Do you do the laundry?"

"Sometimes."

She gives me a look—you know the kind of look I'm talking about.

"Well, I'll take care of the whole thing. I'll build the clothesline."

"Will you really be building the clothesline yourself?" The look has intensified.

"I'll probably hire someone to do it. So I'll be helping the economy." If only I can figure out how the clothesline will help me lose weight, I'd be golden. I suppose I could devise a fun and challenging jogging course in my yard involving the clothesline. Actually, I'd end up on my back, having clothes-lined myself. And then Marla would say "I told you so" and make me take it down. As soon as I recovered from my back-breaking fall.

WEDNESDAY, FEBRUARY 25, 2009

A "new place" is today's theme—*how we end up in a new place when we binge and how we gain new insight into our problem.* When I binge, my new insight tells me I won't eat a whole roll of cookie dough next time.

The only bingeing I've done recently was *Yesterday's Em-panadas.* But once I binged and it saved my life. Here's what happened.

One of the things my wife has me do, and I enjoy hav-ing to do, is going to Costco. I'm very happy there. I love the samples—and if they don't have enough, I end up buying more stuff, for some reason that's the way it works—and I love the simple freedom to purchase many things in bulk. Because if I'm not eating sugar, I need to do something to shove down the feelings. For example, the reason I eat Pop-Tarts raw is that if I have to wait until I toast them, I start feeling feelings. . . . Shopping is a good distraction. However, there's a Krispy Kreme Doughnuts on the way to Costco, and that's the real reason I love going there.

Now, in the past I played a game, a game with one very strict rule to which I always adhered. I only stopped at the Krispy Kreme if the sign that says the donuts are warm and fresh was lit. If the sign wasn't turned on, sorry, no old donuts for me. One day last year I was on my way to Costco and the sign was on. I went in and picked out five donuts. Five being a perfect number, because once you get to six, you start talking in relation to a dozen: half dozen, three-quarters of a dozen. No one ever says five-twelfths of a dozen.

Then I got my skim milk. I had to have the nonfat milk to go with the donuts. And then I sat down. Next to me was a guy who had a plateful of donuts and chocolate milk. And I sat there in judgment thinking, *What kind of idiot drinks chocolate milk with their donuts? That's gluttonous.* I was judging him with five donuts piled up in front of me. And in the world of sugar— know this—in the world of sugar, Krispy Kremes are like her- oin. If you are able to eat just one Krispy Kreme, then you don't know what I'm talking about. If you have two, three, and four, maybe even five—God forbid, six—you enter into a great haze.

So in my great haze I drove over to Costco, and as I was getting close to the store, there were cops everywhere. There were lights flashing, cars pulling in. There was a cop directing traffic. And I said to him, "Hey. Hey, what happened?"

"A guy got shot walking into Costco about ten minutes ago."

"Shot? Is he okay?"

"I don't know."

I was driving home, and all of a sudden it occured to me: Krispy Kreme saved my life. Now, understand, I knew that Krispy Kreme was killing me—I was well aware of that—but death by donuts is much slower than by a bullet.

But here's the crazy thing. This wasn't the first strange sign from above delivered to me via a Krispy Kreme donut. Bear with me.

I play golf on occasion. I don't have time to play that often, and I'm not very good, but I actually enjoy being out amongst the trees. (A golf course is all the nature I can handle.) But I do like walking around. It's nice, especially on a cool day, you know? If it's too hot, I'm not playing. But in California we have a lot of nice, cool mornings.

I also get invited to a lot of celebrity golf tournaments. And they always give out free stuff, usually golf clubs or something like that. But I went to this one tournament, and at every hole they served fresh Krispy Kreme donuts. I didn't eat any for seventeen holes. I got to the eighteenth hole and thought, *All right. Look what you just did, that's fantastic. Such self-control. You can have one.* Those of us with these big eating disorders have these inner monologues. *You can have one. Go ahead and have one.* So I took one. I was going to love it. I was going to eat it very slowly.

Generally, I eat fast. I was going to eat this one very slowly. I opened my mouth and took a bite. A bee flew into my mouth, stung the roof of my mouth, and fell dead on the ground. I finished chewing the donut, through the pain. It felt like the moment the dentist first injects the Novocain, before it numbs your mouth. It was like that for about an hour. I thought it was

God sending a message, saying, "Don't you remember when you were in that room with all that wedding food? You should have stopped then." So I went a long time before eating another Krispy Kreme. But I did it once again. I receive the warnings, and well, you know. Logic has absolutely nothing to do with compulsive overeating. I wish it did. I'd be healthy.

11

Here's what I've done to make my house more environmentally friendly since my visit to Ed Begley Jr.'s house: nothing.

Well, that's not true. I've called Residential Energy Assessment Services (REAS), the company Ed suggested to do the physical on my house. Meanwhile, my wife still hasn't embraced my whole green thing. She wishes the book were just about me losing weight. In fact, she and I are engaged in a Battle Royale about replacing the windows, something I've wanted to do since I went to Ed's house.

Marla actually thinks, and I'm not making this up, that our house will begin to fall apart if we install new windows. I want her to be here when Ed comes over, since he is so inspiring. Ed's a little late and she wants to leave; she has errands to do and she's antsy. I ask for her to be patient. Finally Ed arrives. He's so disarming and charming that I don't worry about Marla's anxiety.

"Where do you want to start, Ed?" I ask. "We can go

through the whole house—outside, inside—because I want your opinion of everything."

"Let's start out front," he says.

But when we go outside, the guys have arrived to mow the lawn. They've got the leaf blowers going now. You can't hear anything. Plus, after seeing Ed's fake grass, I know that lawns aren't green, if you know what I mean. "I can have them stop for about twenty minutes," I say, a little embarrassed.

"You know what Jeff wants to do?" Marla says to Ed. "He wants to get rid of all the grass and do something ecologically sound." I step away to go over to the guys. I figure that when I get back, Ed will have made more progress with Marla in three minutes than I have in three months.

I come back. "He's gonna turn that off. I mean, there's no reason he can't rake. Lawn mowers are horrible for the environment." Of course, it's never really occurred to me before, but with Ed standing here at my house, it's the most obvious thing in the world.

"Some of these gardeners will make a change if you ask them," Ed tells us. "They may charge a little more to rake."

"Well, I think our gardener will have to make the adjustment. He's good; he'll make the adjustment. I've got to give him the opportunity to do it the right way."

"What if we just buy the right tools for our gardener to use at our house?" asks Marla.

"That's what I did at first," says Ed. "The guy I have now has all that stuff. But I'm sure you don't want to cost a man his job over the equipment, so I'm all for keeping your guy. Also, there are different kinds of grasses that require less water. And this is something that Ron and Tammy (the people from REAS) will help you with. I'm not sure what kind of lawn this is, but it doesn't look like the most drought tolerant kind of lawn. There are some native grasses that need a lot less water. Take a look at those; make sure they're aesthetically pleasing. At one point I ended up with the Addams Family yard. I was taking care of it, but then I got busy and slacked off on the upkeep. I didn't even see it happen, but it turned into tumbleweeds. You might consider putting a gray-water system in your house. Then you take all that water from your shower, washer and dryer, and your bathroom sink, and you water your lawn with it. Not the kitchen sink; that has ground-up stuff in it. You can't have that. You obviously can't have it from toilets; that's called black water."

The concept of gray water is disturbing enough, but there is no way I'm going to walk on my own doody. I deal enough with the dogs pooping everywhere.

As we go around the outside of our house, Ed points to the windows. Thank God. "These kinds of windows are single pane, and they don't always have the best seal. You're hemorrhaging heat and money right there. But you can replace them; they make ones now that will look quite similar."

"They have a horrible seal. We know that," I say, gloating.

"Jeff must have begged you to come over and make comments about the windows so that I would agree to get rid of them," Marla says, sensing a setup.

"I'm sorry," Ed says. I can tell that he realizes he's gotten himself into something.

"Did I ever mention anything to you about the windows ahead of time?"

"Never did," says Ed.

"Never said a word," I insist.

"I swear it to you," says Ed.

"You don't understand," I tell Marla. "We can get windows that look similar, that will give us better protection."

"That is true," Ed agrees. "If you don't want to make the jump to replacing all of them, since that's going to be a big-ticket item—"

"I know it is," I interrupt. "But it's an important one." I'm dead set on winning this one.

"It is very important," says Ed.

Finally Marla speaks up. "Maybe we do the bottom floor first, then the top." I've been working on her about these windows for three months. Ed's got her convinced in less than three minutes.

"There you go," says Ed. "You don't run up Mount Everest. One step at a time, you get to base camp, you get acclimated, then you go a little higher. That's what you do. You don't want to make yourself crazy. Your marriage, your physical and mental well-being is part of the ecosystem, too. You've got to factor that in."

I look at Marla and then at Ed. He couldn't be more right. I think the world of Ed Begley.

"We want to put in a vegetable garden," says Marla. Now, the garden is something we are both excited about. "We want to hire someone to help us. I mean, I want to do it with my kids, but I think that we should hire someone to guide us."

"Definitely do this," Ed encourages her. "Money well spent. When you are first doing a garden, you want to get some help. You can do lettuce and herbs over there," says Ed, pointing to an area near the house. "That's a good place for cool-weather stuff. Then this," he gestures down the hill, "gets a little more tricky. This is going to get leaves in the spring and summer. I haven't seen a place that gets really good sun so far—for corn and tomatoes, you need a lot of sun."

We're walking around the yard now, and I almost step on one of my dog Bella's poops. Of course. "Can we recycle that?" I ask, totally kidding.

"Sadly, no. I tried," says Ed. Of course he has attempted to recycle dog poop! "There is a way to do it, but I recommend against it. I used to have a Doggie Dooley, which is like a doggy septic tank. I had it for a while, and it worked great at first. But then a very bad thing happened—it turned very ugly. I'll spare you the details. It turned real bad." The expression on his face tells me that I do not want to ask any more questions.

"What about in here for a garden?" asks Marla. "It's actually the dog area now."

"Perfect. Here's where you want to put your tomatoes and stuff. Just start small. You'll take a little space away from the dogs, but they'll still have plenty of room."

"If we put in the drought-tolerant grass, can the dogs run on that? Because these girls destroy our grass."

"They can run on it. They'll love it," says Ed.

"Good. I think that's what we have to do." Really, this seems completely doable.

Next, we go into the kitchen and Ed takes a look at our appliances.

"The stove is fine; it's electric. You know, some people find it harder to cook with electric. I have gas now, but I had electric for a while. The timing's a little different when you're turning a knob to adjust a flame versus a heat coil. But the good thing about electric is, you can certainly buy green electricity from the Department of Water and Power and that's less CO_2, and less pollution."

"I didn't know we could do that. Marla, will you make a note?"

"There's a check box on your bill from the DWP, or at least there used to be one. If not, just call them up and ask for their green power program. It costs a little bit more, but then it's green power that you are using to cook your food. It's not coal, it's not nuclear; it's wind/solar/geothermal that you are using to cook your food. Same with your fridge. Have you had this fridge for a while?"

"We've had it for about five years."

"Five years, keep using it. But when you're ready to replace, let's say five years from now, then you get one of the really energy efficient refrigerators. But this is fine for now. It's like if somebody's driving around in a car that gets decent mileage and decides to put it in a scrap heap and get a Prius—that's a mistake. It took a lot of energy to make that car, and getting rid of it in favor of a hybrid kind of defeats the purpose.

"It's true. People throw out perfectly good things and spend more money than they need to in the name of being green.

Given what goes into making a Prius, you're not doing anybody any favors by getting rid of a car that gets decent mileage. Ride that other pony out until it's really done. And then you can get your Prius.

We come to the same conclusion about the washer and dryer, which are also just five years old. Now is my chance to bring up the clothesline, another issue of contention between my wife and me. Poor Ed, he's in the middle of the Marla-and-Jeff-Garlin cross fire.

"I was also thinking about hanging a clothesline in front here, off the wall."

"Do it! It's great," says Ed. "I had a clothesline as a kid. That's what we used. The clothes come out great! And it saves so much energy. It's such a great alternative for all the things that are not a rush."

"That's what I've been saying to you, Marla," I say.

"It dries so quickly," says Ed.

"Okay," says Marla.

Okay? Are you kidding? Have I really won this battle, too? "Well, that was easy," I say, but then I wonder, what happens when Ed goes home?

We go inside. "Now, do you unplug everything?" I ask Ed. This is something I've been wondering about.

"I have a GreenSwitch, so I don't have to. You can get a GreenSwitch system, where just one click of the switch when you go to bed or leave the house turns off all the vampire power."

"Wow! How is it that you don't know about this?" Marla asks. She's totally into this.

"This is why Ed's here! GreenSwitch. It's wireless throughout the house?"

"It's wireless. You can order switches online, and your electrician will install them for you. Here's the beauty of the GreenSwitch. If you want to turn off all the lights with one flick of the switch, that's called a full GreenSwitch. Let's say you're about to go out, but you're expecting a fax. You can do a half and half—half GreenSwitch, half solid on. You can leave it on that setting if you need your fax machine to stay on all the time. Your clock radio, your DVD player, whatever stuff you pick can be set half and half on the same outlet. They have them in hotels all over Europe, because guests were always leaving everything on. So you leave the house, boink. You go to bed, boink."

"That's great," I say.

"Genius," agrees Marla.

They could call it the boinker.

As we start heading down to the basement, my phone rings. I look at my caller ID. It says Flake Wilkerson. "Who's Flake Wilkerson? Somebody named Flake Wilkerson is calling me." I have no idea who Flake Wilkerson is.

"With a name like that, we have to pick it up," says Marla.

I answer the phone. Flake Wilkerson asks for Jeff Garlin.

"This is me," I say. Turns out it's AT&T, going under the alias Flake Wilkerson. I'm not making this up. Flake asks me to participate in a survey. I decline the request and hang up.

"Flake Wilkerson is AT&T for a survey," I say.

"Unbelievable," says Ed. I'm about to go off on the

number of unsolicited calls we get even though we signed up for the no-call list, when Ed suddenly exclaims, "Oh! Wait a minute . . . weather stripping." He's feeling around our basement. "I can feel it, right here. This stuff you can do while you're waiting for those windows. Ron and Tammy Schwolsky can get a team to come in, and they'll be able to do something for you right away for those gaps within a week! For not a lot of money."

"What about our water heater?" asks Marla, leading him to a storage area off the basement.

He takes a look and says, "Okay, here's another big savings for you. You're going to get rid of this water heater. It won't go into a landfill. The plumber will give it to somebody, sell it to somebody, whatever—there's somebody who will love this. You're going to get an A. O. Smith. It's an American company, been around for a hundred years, and they make the A. O. Smith Vertex One Hundred. It's ninety-six percent thermal efficiency. I've got one at my house, so you know it's good. You're gonna save so much natural gas with that."

"That's a good one. We'll definitely get that," says Marla. "Just so you know, everything in my house is pretty much recyclable."

"I love it," says Ed.

"I pride myself on buying things from my friends—I recover, I redo. I'm all about that," says Marla.

"I can see. Look at this beautiful thing," he says, moving toward an antique dresser.

"Well, I actually bought that piece, but it's an exception . . . very few things are new in our house."

She's full of shit. We have bought plenty of new things. I think my wife is in love with Ed Begley.

"That's great," says Ed.

"I feel really good about that," says Marla.

"You should."

There's a pause, as Marla basks in his approval of her sudden commitment to the cause. I interrupt her reverie: "Yeah, and this couch is made out of milk cartons."

She shoots me a look, you know the one, and then we head upstairs to show Ed the bathroom that we're redoing. He compliments us on our energy-saving thermostat on our way up the stairs, but then Marla has to tell him that it's actually our alarm. I explain that the bathroom is the one room in the house that's falling apart. It's outdated. We're going to put in a shower with a glass partition, a new tub, a low-flow toilet, a sink, maybe even two sinks.

"Do two," Ed says. "Two's always good. In a marriage, it's good to have two sinks."

He's not the first person to tell us this. Everyone says you have to put in two sinks. My wife and I have been sharing a sink for fourteen years, and never once has there been a sink-related fight. But I'm starting to get the feeling that there are sink fights happening all over the country.

"We're thinking about getting a steam shower. Is that a bad thing?"

"No. Get some steam. Have your luxuries. Have some steam. It's fine. With the A. O. Smith, you get it from a reliable, energy efficient source."

"Great. Is there any kind of special tub we should get, or any sort of materials we should consider using?"

"Yeah," says Ed. "Some materials are greener than others. Ron and Tammy will tell you about them. There's something called Vetrazzo. It's made from recycled Coke bottles. And recycled glass from old lenses from traffic lights, from glass from an office building in San Francisco; it's amazing stuff. I have it in my kitchen. It's beautiful. And it's recyclable."

"This is all very exciting, just making my life lighter," I say, and I mean it. Ed's an inspiration. He walks the walk; that's what drew me to him. Maybe if I can show people how easy some of this stuff is, I can set an example, too. People don't look at me as a guy who would do this type of stuff. So that's my hope. If a guy like me, who loves his air-conditioning and stays away from nature, can contribute to a cleaner planet, so can anyone.

Is it working yet?

12

Tonight I tell the audience at my Sunday UCB show that I'm going to take the bus to the set. The green part of my plan is really starting to happen. I'm feeling proud of myself—no one takes the bus in L.A.! I'm talking about taking it once, as an experiment. I feel a collective shrug from the audience, a shrug that says, "That's not such a big deal." I say, "Yeah, you're right. I'll take it a few times." Once again, a mountain of indifference. Then I ask them, "How many of you take the bus on a regular basis?" Quite a few hands go up. I feel like an arrogant asshole. So I ask, "What if I take it for a month?" I got a big round of applause. The decision is made.

I go home and order a monthly pass online for the month of April. It's easy and fun. I can't believe I had fun ordering a bus pass. But I'm getting excited about doing something new to lower my carbon footprint. Now I can't wait to get started. I wish it were April. I'm going to take the bus every day, everywhere I go, for the entire month. I'll leave my car in the driveway, and that means I'll have to walk almost a mile to the bus stop. It's going to be a pain in the ass, but I'm doing it, because it's good. It's good for everyone.

MONDAY, MARCH 2, 2009

Today's message from my book of meditations is about changing—how when we're losing weight, we can be a bit *fearful of the change*. I'm not scared of change. I don't feel a thing.

"It was a big part of your life to not take such good care of yourself," George Shapiro, Jerry Seinfeld's manager, says to me today, as we're sitting next to each other. And he's right; it was a big part of my life. Truthfully, it *was* my life. Maybe I was more afraid of change than I thought.

Today the cast of *Seinfeld* joins our cast. Part of the storyline for this season is a *Seinfeld* reunion. The first thing we are filming is a table read. For this scene, Larry has assembled not only the original cast, but also the writers and the crew. We are filming this on the same soundstage at CBS Radford that *Seinfeld* was filmed on, and we're using the original sets from the show. It's all rather surreal. Jerry tells me to keep on doing *Curb*—don't stop until Larry's done.

I'm not stupid.

TUESDAY, MARCH 3, 2009

Today's meditation is about precision, about being precise when we measure our food. I've always felt that I may be more precise when I measure my food, but also more obsessive. My goal is to not obsess about food in any way. I just want to eat healthily and not worry about it. Just do it.

Back on the soundstage, more scenes on the *Seinfeld* set. Every day I'm having lunch with the *Seinfeld* cast. Again, it's all so surreal. And by the way, all the *Seinfeld* people are completely intrigued by my weight loss and green initiative. They can't ask me enough questions. Every day for lunch I eat a salad out of a big wooden bowl, the kind you'd use to serve a salad at the dinner table. I eat a monster salad for lunch. The most-high calorie thing that I occasionally put in there are black olives, which are high in fat, but that's the wildest shit that I put in my salad. There's no cheese. There's no Thousand Island. But I do know that no matter what you put in a salad, people see you eating salad and they say, "Oh, look at you! That's very impressive." You could have a nine thousand-calorie salad, and people would say, "Good for you."

Also, today Jerry's assistant, Melissa, introduces me to an application for my iPhone called Lose It! If you put your weight, physical activities, and what you eat into Lose It!, you can keep track of your calories and how long it should take you to lose your weight. I love technology.

Speaking of technology, I just bought a luxury item that I am thrilled with. I'm not a guy who drives fancy cars and lives the high life. I make a good living, but I'm not rich. This is something I've dreamed about getting for years, and I haven't done it until now. I finally said to myself, it's time.

I'm a large man and I like my water. For weight loss, it's key. For nice breath, key. For just functioning and not feeling tired, key. So I had a reverse osmosis system put in!

With this reverse osmosis system, I just flip a switch and get my own clean and delicious water. All of the contaminants—particles, sediments, elements that even bottled water contain—are filtered out. Not only am I saving a fortune on buying drinking water, but there are no plastics to recycle. I feel like the king of the world every time I flip the switch. My son had some friends over today, and I actually asked one of the parents, "Can I offer you some reverse osmosis water?" I could've been a great reverse osmosis system salesman. I can't get enough of it. Actually, I should thank my wife. She gave me permission to buy it.

WEDNESDAY, MARCH 4, 2009

Today's meditation is all about doing what feels good and how the initial pleasure of overeating ultimately turns to pain. *Doing anything as long as it feels good is a trap.*

I'm Jewish; I don't know from doing what feels good until it turns to pain. I stop a few seconds into pleasure, think about it, and then I feel immense guilt.

Today we're filming all the "rehearsal" scenes for the *Seinfeld* reunion. It's all very exciting, however, it's becoming a bit of a challenge for me to stay sober. One of the reasons is that, as I've said, I'm frustrated with the way we shoot things. I know what we need to get, and when we get it, we should move on. We're shooting too many takes. Nobody's making choices. All this extra shooting for no reason makes me crazy. Crazy and bored. And when I'm bored, I eat. I'm filled with anxiety because, for once, I'm not in denial. I'm trying to stay sober, to stay off the sugar. Staying sober means feeling shitty. It's not my body, it's my mind. It's crazy. If I eat shit, my body feels poorly. If I eat healthy food, my mind feels poorly. I'm starting to feel like I can't function without medication. Self-medication. I need sugar. Well, I want sugar.

Another problem is that I don't have much to do. I'm not really in any scenes, and my expertise as a director is being ignored. Now that I'm off sugar, I really feel it when I'm bored with my job. Like George Shapiro said, "It was a big part of your life not to take such good care of yourself."

THURSDAY, MARCH 5, 2009

Today's message is about *old tapes*. Something about the recesses of our minds and old tapes stored away. I don't get this.

I have been a dick for about two or three weeks. Actually, I've been a dick for a couple of months. I've been snapping at everyone I work with, and this is not normal behavior for me. It's not nice, and I'm convinced it comes from eating well. If I were having Pop-Tarts and shoving down the feelings, well then, the world knows there's nothing like a jolly fat man. Filled with white flour and sugar, I was a doll. And by the way, I am an apology machine because, with every one of those dick things that I've done, I've apologized for them within five minutes. "Oh, fuck. Did I just . . . ? Oh, man, I'm sorry." People are getting sick of my apologizing.

Here's the thing: you start eating right, you exercise, you start taking care of yourself, and then, before you know it, you're skipping exercising and grabbing whatever food is nearby. But what I've come to learn is, all these things that you have to feel are there every day. They don't go away just because you've been taking such good care of yourself.

Meanwhile, the *Seinfeld* people remain obsessed by my weight loss. Jerry Seinfeld has got a sadistic side to him, and he enjoys talking about things he's eaten, especially, it seems, when I'm around.

Today I'm at lunch with Jerry, Jason, Michael, and Julia. They're asking me all sorts of questions about my diet. And Jerry says, "Hey, if you could eat anything, what would you eat?"

"A cheeseburger and a chocolate milk shake."

Then he turns to his manager and says, "George, did I not say I'm getting that tonight?" The thing is, he isn't kidding.

About four hours later it's the afternoon and I'm planning on having some plain yogurt shortly. Some fruit. Something extremely boring, crazy boring. Jerry Seinfeld comes up to me and says, "Garlin, what are you going to do about the pizza?" As soon as he says it, the pizza smell hits my nose. I didn't even know they were serving pizza, and I'm not going to go near it. "What are you going to do about the pizza?" he persists.

"Well, I hadn't noticed the pizza until you said that." Didn't I tell you he is sadistic? "I'm not going to even have the pizza." I walk away, and then my assistant comes up to me and says— and this is crossing the line, as far as I'm concerned—"I don't want you to have any of that pizza. Can I go get you some fruit?" If I wanted her to get me some pizza with some chocolate sauce on it, she's going to go do that. I have a wife and I have a mother and I have a bunch of doctors. I don't need someone else saying to me, especially when I'm grumpy, "I don't want you to have any of that pizza. Can I get you some fruit?"

"No, I'm fine," I say. "Trust me, I'm not going anywhere near that pizza." But soon I find myself in close proximity to the pizza; in fact, I'm walking toward the pizza, but I have no intention of eating it, really. The craft service woman, who's in charge of getting the food for the set, sees me and says, "We got you the pizza without the cheese."

"Oh, really?" So I walk over to check it out, even though I know it's going to look shitty. Also, it's made with white flour. I shouldn't have it. But everyone around me is eating pizza—pizza that actually looks good. They're about to start shooting a scene, so everyone runs to the set. Everyone. I'm standing by myself, surrounded by at least twenty boxes of pizza. There's some Hawaiian pizza, which has pineapple and ham on it. I was planning on becoming a vegetarian today. So all right, I'll pull off the ham and I'll have one of those. Boy, the pineapple's good. You know, it's fruity and good. I end up having six slices of pizza, all in row, standing there by myself.

I'm not beating myself up. I'm pretty cool. I've switched gears and I'm in a much better mood. I think to myself, *it happens*. At least I haven't eaten cookies or any of that stuff: no Pop-Tarts. So fine, I ate six slices of pizza and now it's over.

I start walking back to the set after they've shot the scene, and Jerry comes up to me. "Hey, you want to go to Jerry's Deli (It's actually called Jerry's Famous Deli, having nothing to do with Jerry Seinfeld except that he likes it) tonight with Larry, George, and me?"

"Yeah, I'll go to Jerry's Deli. Sure, sure."

Then Jerry says, "I'm warning you: I'm getting a cheeseburger and a chocolate milk shake."

"I know, I know." I'm pretty sure he's serious, because, as I said, he's sadistsic. I start thinking ahead of time: planning, because I know I'm not going to get a cheeseburger. What am I going to get? The problem is that at Jerry's, there's nothing for me to eat, and the food sucks anyway. Jerry Seinfeld loves it, but it's bad. I'm standing there strategizing about what I will eat at Jerry's when Larry David calls out to me from across the set and says, "Come here."

"What?"

"Come with me."

So I follow him into his dressing room, and he says, "You're not eating enough. Here. Have some sushi."

"No. I'm stuffed."

"Come on, you're doing so good. Have some sushi."

"All right, I'll have a piece."

"Have one of those rice things." If one more piece of sushi goes in me, I am going to throw up. You don't want to be vomiting sushi and Hawaiian pizza.

"Please, no more," I say, as if I'm a torture victim. "I'm going to Jerry's."

"Oh, good. Good. You'll eat later."

That night at Jerry's, George orders a cheeseburger. Jerry orders a bacon cheeseburger, a milk shake, curly fries, *and* steak fries. Larry orders something pretty healthy and doesn't eat too much. I order soup, but when you get soup in a restaurant, there's way too much sodium. So I get a cup of hot water with my bowl of soup, and pour the hot water into the soup. It still tastes crazy salty to someone who's been on a low-salt diet for months. Of course, everyone's watching me, and they're very impressed.

Now, I swear to God, the one person aside from maybe my parents and my wife who wants me to get healthy the most is Larry. He's the most encouraging and supportive of my efforts. He doesn't want me to stay fat. People always assume that for the show he wants me to be fat—you know, because of Susie calling me a fat fuck and all that insulting stuff. Once, Larry said to me, and it was a great compliment, "You don't need to be fat to be funny. That's not how you're funny. You could be funny at any weight." But he has to leave dinner early, and I'm left alone with George and Jerry the Sadist.

As soon as Larry leaves, Jerry orders a giant cookie cream thing. After the chocolate milk shake and a bacon cheeseburger and a lot of fries. I have that calorie counting thing on my iPhone, and Jerry wants to know how many calories he's eaten. We're figuring out his calories, and then suddenly I have the urge to come clean—I tell him about the six slices of pizza. He roars with laughter.

As I drive home, I'm pleased that at least I'm a vegetarian. Fine, doubt me.

FRIDAY, MARCH 6, 2009

Today's meditation is about living now and how when you eat compulsively, you aren't in the *here and now*. If I'm not here, not now, then where am I? Organizing tapes in the recesses of my mind? I'm getting a little frustrated with these meditations.

Today I'm standing around futzing with my iPhone between takes we're filming in the parking lot by Moca Joe's cart on the Radford lot. Here's my problem with the Lose It! app. I keep on deleting it and reinstalling it. Not because there's a problem with the technology, but because every time I eat something bad I want to start over. I dutifully enter my transgression and then immediately want to erase the evidence and pretend it didn't happen.

I get home and check the mail for my bus pass. It hasn't arrived. I feel like a kid waiting for the decoder ring he ordered from a cereal box.

SUNDAY, MARCH 8, 2009
Weigh-in time . . .
Weight: 268
Blood Sugar: 118
Wii Fit age: 51

My blood sugar is up a little. Also, I'm getting a little suspicious of this Wii Fit age thing. Before you know it I'll be ninety. And maybe I should think about using the Wii Fit for something other than measuring my weight and mysteriously calculating my age. Like maybe some exercise. SARAH JESSICA PARKER.

13

TUESDAY, MARCH 10, 2009

Ron, Tammy, and Josh Gould come over today. They did our comprehensive energy audit a few weeks ago, and now they have the results to discuss with Marla and me. We looked at the report together and I recorded the conversation. The transcript is sixty-five pages long. You can thank me now for sparing you from that. But knowledge is the first step in making changes, so I thought I'd share the crucial eco-terms I learned from the assessment.

Air leakage. This is a big deal. Ron, Tammy, and Josh must have used the words "air leakage" fifteen times. The good news is my chimney dampers really aren't that bad, compared to most people's. (Chimneys are bad for air leakage, if that wasn't obvious.) My chimneys are "pretty tight." Ron told us to get some kind of fancy ornament to hang from the handle of the damper to remind us to open the flue before starting a fire. This was funny because we've been living in this house for five years and we haven't built a fire yet. Which is apparently a good thing because Tammy told me that burning wood is not good for indoor air quality, and that in L.A. they won't let you do a new construction with a wood-burning fireplace anymore.

Plastic bladder. Josh explained it like this: "To ensure that your chimney is airtight, you actually stick this deflated bladder into the chimney, and then you blow on this thing through a tube until it becomes extremely tight, like a balloon that takes the shape of the chimney and creates an air seal. Then you disconnect your blow-up hose and just leave it alone. And it's out of sight, out of mind—and rest assured that it's airtight." So I guess I'm going to shove a plastic bladder up my chimney. I feel like I've been talking to a urologist.

Weather stripping. Mentioned almost as many times as **air leakage.** Possibly because it prevents **air leakage.**

Thermal envelope. A small, cozy, well-conditioned living area created by preventing **air leakage** through **weather stripping.** Obviously.

Mountainous areas and low valleys. Believe it or not, this is how Ron described the insulation in my attic. You do not want mountainous areas and low valleys in your attic. You want "uniform, even coverage throughout all areas."

Any hole in the wall. By definition, must be removed. Holes in the wall create **air leakage,** i.e., via an unused air conditioner in our upstairs bedroom. A hole in the wall is removed by throwing insulation into it.

Vapor area. Tammy suggested installing one in the crawl space that's behind the HVAC system. She told me to "layer really thick plastic and heat it up in the walls, and that will keep either the moisture or the dust or everything sealed down." I said, "Right, right," but I had no idea what she was talking about, so that's why this isn't much of a definition. I mask my incomprehension by saying, "Just know that I am thoroughly enjoying this part." Ron replied, "You're the first customer we've had that's enjoyed this part." And Tammy added, "Well, watch out. We're just on the first phase. We've got two-thirds to go."

"Your house sucks." Apparently Ron and Tammy have to tell this to people all the time. "Well," Tammy said to me, "your house isn't bad; we're not actually gonna tell you yours sucks."

New windows. Get them! Ron, Tammy, and Josh are totally on my side. Ron said that our windows are "old, uncomfortable, and poorly operating." Unfortunately, he said this at 9:55 a.m., and my wife "thought" the meeting started at ten. New windows eliminate **air leakage.**

Combustion air inlet pipe. A pipe Josh recommend I install from the outside of the house leading into the sealed combustion-burning chamber of the furnace, in order to pull in clean air from outside, as opposed to taking air from inside, which apparently could be introducing microorganisms and dust into our living space. Benefit: extends longevity of furnace and uses "better air." Caution: "special cap" must be purchased to make sure that bees and birds don't end up frying in sealed combustion burning chamber. Why is it a "special cap"? The regular cap should be called "the bird murderer."

78/68. The temperatures to which the state of California recommends you set your thermostat. That would be seventy-eight degrees in summer and sixty-eight degrees in the winter. Upon learning this, Marla (who did arrive at 10:00 a.m.) exclaimed, "I never knew that! We reverse it. We're completely reversed!"

Fans. Here's a news flash: "Fans are only about cooling the skin, the human skin," said Tammy. The cooling effect of the fan is due to the evaporation of the moisture on the surface of your skin. When a fan is on, and nobody is in the room, it's actually creating heat, because of the motor from the fan. You should know that I am the king of the bedroom fan. It is always on. I don't want to believe them on this one.

Dual flush. Water-efficient toilets. This seems like an easy thing to do—replace all the toilets in the house. But Ron warned me: "It's a different kind of flush. The first time you flush it, you're going to think, Is there something wrong with the toilet? It's a pretty powerful flush."

Second refrigerator. An energy hog. You gotta get rid of that, they told us. You can imagine how I feel about this. Marla said,

"Okay. I don't always need it. But we're having a party tonight. That's when I use it. Can I unplug it? And just plug it in when I need it? We're having a bar mitzvah soon, too." There's always something.

Carbon footprint calculation. The Nature Conservancy has a website that will calculate your carbon footprint based on a series of questions that Ron and Tammy, in turn, asked me. Turns out ours is "way lower" than the average. I started getting pretty excited, but Tammy wouldn't let me gloat for too long. "Well, this is one calculation. I wouldn't take this as the bible of your carbon footprint at this point." Ron went on to talk about what your utility company uses to generate electricity and how that skews your carbon footprint, and how there are distribution losses over the line. Whatever. I'm feeling like I just got on the scale and found out I was thirty pounds lighter than I thought I was.

Deconstruction. When the contractor comes to get started on the bathroom, we're not supposed to use the word "demolition." Tammy told us that deconstruction is what we want. Demolition means smashing everything apart. With deconstruction, they save all the old stuff and donate it. Habitat for Humanity's one of the best places to give fixtures, sinks, and things like that. They won't take your non-low-flow toilets, though. But don't worry, Ed Begley recycles them into pants.

Nervous breakdown. This is what my wife is about to have, after learning everything we need to do to our house, as in,

"Oh God. I'm about to have a nervous breakdown, I really am. I just have to let you know this. Tuesday, I start my bathroom. And my kids are on spring break, and I have no nanny. It's just me, and I have to get my invitations out this week for the bar mitzvah. I need to know how long this is going to take. How long is this process?"

As I said, the transcript was boring, but actually, things got a little heated toward the end. I submit the following section of transcript to you, the reader, as evidence. You'll understand once you've finished the book. The following occurred when we asked Ron and Tammy for advice about remodeling our bathroom in a green fashion. They suggested, as you know, re-cycling the old bathroom fixtures (remember, "deconstruct," don't demolish).

MARLA: What if my contractor says to me, We don't do this stuff, it takes too much time?

TAMMY: Contractors need every job they can get.

JEFF: But you need to call him now and not wait until he gets here.

MARLA: I'm going to call him today.

RON: The thing is, you have to at least ask. It never hurts to ask. You say, "You know, what do you do with all the old parts?" And if he's forward thinking, he'll say something like, "This is something I should have thought of myself."

MARLA: It would probably make him more business.

RON: Totally. He'll have you as a reference, saying he took care of you.

JEFF: So you are taking care of this, I don't need to—

MARLA: Okay. Just as long as I get my drapes.

JEFF: You didn't ask me about the drapes.

MARLA: No. Measurements were taken, but I haven't gotten anything yet.

JEFF: Somebody came and measured?

MARLA: I haven't even done anything.

JEFF: You just told me measurements were taken; that's something. . . . I don't know anything.

MARLA: Well, pay attention.

RON: Jeff, you're okay because she's not going to hang any drapes at least until the new windows are in.

MARLA: Yeah, I'm not doing anything yet.

RON: So you bought a few months.

MARLA: I'm not doing anything yet.

JEFF: Yeah. Okay. So we'll do all that. But. Here's the thing that I don't want ignored. The bathroom. I don't know who's coming here, who's involved.

MARLA: You're not home.

JEFF: I don't need to be, is what I'm saying.

MARLA: Okay, you're going to witness a fight here.

JEFF: No, you're not.

TAMMY: We're all married here.

MARLA: What do you need to know, Jeff? What is it that you're needing to know?

JEFF: You're not letting me speak! Holy crap! Okay. There must be a checklist of things you need to ask them, and have done, for the bathroom.

MARLA: Right.

JEFF: It's not about just letting them come in, and they use formaldehyde on everything. I need you to have a checklist of things you need to ask them.

MARLA: I've already asked them.

JEFF: And you got the information?

MARLA: Yeah, he wrote it down. I have all the information.

JEFF: Who's he?

MARLA: Our contractor.

JEFF: So, basically, the contractor has told you what questions to ask him?

MARLA: No. Jeff, this is not a conversation for right now. I will take care of it. I already talked to him about the installation. He uses a special installation that—

JEFF: What is it? I want to know what it is. You're telling me that your contractor's telling you he's good?

MARLA: Just know that I have it taken care of.

JEFF: No, you don't have it taken care of.

MARLA: You're not home, Jeff.

JEFF: You're not hearing what I'm saying. You need to have a checklist.

MARLA: I understand.

JEFF: Admit you learned a lot today.

MARLA: I admit that I learned a lot.

JEFF: Okay, thank you. Yeah.

MARLA: Our house will be green, although we'll be divorced. That's the new name for your book! *Green Is My Divorce!*

14

Today's meditation is about vulnerability. *How when we stop overeating, we become vulnerable. Food has stood in the way of our feelings.* Correct. Food has stood in the way of all my feelings.

Today is a driving shot of Larry dressed in an early-sixties period costume. Today is also bowl of yogurt day. I don't stop. It's healthier than eating pizza. Progress, not perfection.

WEDNESDAY, MARCH 18, 2009

Today is all about a new world, *by being honest and abstinent, we are thrown into a new world.*

We're filming *Curb Your Enthusiasm* in Brentwood today—we film in Brentwood a lot—and whenever we do any scenes of driving or we're on the street, we have cops who control the traffic. Actually, we have cops when we're on any set. They're usually guys who are retired or about to be retired. It's a cush gig, to be a cop on a set.

There's one guy who is a couple years younger than me, and a little bit shorter than me, and he weighs about the same as me. He doesn't look obese, but he doesn't look fit. He's not one of those people who you see and think, *Geez, that guy is huge*. Even overweight people think that when they see truly obese people. He wasn't a "geez." My sense is he is a guy who eats a lot.

One day he says to me, "You know, I've been meaning to talk to you. You look great."

"Oh, thank you."

"You've lost weight; you look good."

"Well, thank you very much."

"I just had four stents put in and they told me I may have to have open heart surgery." And he goes on to tell me his whole medical story. I listen; I'm empathetic.

"What are you doing to do lose weight?" he asks.

"Well, I eat really well and I exercise. And that's really all."

"Really?"

"I'm going to tell you something. You can do it." And then I tell him in detail what I do.

"I'm eating a lot of protein bars," he says.

"Don't touch them. They're loaded with sugar. You don't want to mess with protein bars."

"I like a good burger."

"Burgers are no good, either."

"But what about pasta?"

"No pasta. No pasta, none of it. You've got to eat fresh salads and fruit and all sorts of things that are not processed. Stay away from animal fats, and salt, and sugar, and all sorts of processed sugar." I'm feeling even sorrier for this guy—he has no clue what he's up against, what he has to do. "The key thing," I say, "is that it's really hard to do. It's hard. But you can do it. That's the thing nobody tells you. They say, 'Oh, do this trick, do that trick.' No. It's fucking hard, but you can do it."

After we talk, this guy is pumped. He's ready.

I don't see him for the rest of the day. In the afternoon I mosey over to craft service, and there's nothing that I can eat. My friend Zeke, the one from Pritikin whose name isn't really Zeke but asked to be called Zeke in this book, turned me on to Chocolate Chip Clif Bars. No, they're not Snickers bars, but they are loaded with sugar. Yet people think they're healthy, eating these delicious sugary bars. At least they don't make outrageous health claims on the wrapper, like, say, Honey Nut Cheerios, which is my kids' favorite cereal. On the box it says, "May lower cholesterol." What kind of statement is that? Is that even a statement? "It may. We don't know. Do you know? Who are you to argue? It may. It could clear your skin. It could. You don't know." They should just put on the box, "In the future, this could be money. It could. Who knows?"

I wasn't eating any sugar whatsoever when Zeke told me about Chocolate Chip Clif Bars. "Oh, I just have one a day," he said.

But I'm not wired to have only one a day. I wouldn't be fat

if I were. I'm not capable of one-a-day anything. Except for maybe a grapefruit. So there's nothing I can eat at craft services, and the fat cop has got me thinking about Chocolate Chip Clif Bars. Right near where we're filming is a GNC nutrition shop. I walk in, and my energy's low, and I say to the guy who's working there, "Do you have any Clif Bars? Preferably Chocolate Chip?"

"I think over there," he says. I'm looking around for the Clif Bars, and across the store the fat cop is standing, eating a salad out of a container. He's clearly been inspired by our discussion and is eating a salad and looking for vitamins. Meanwhile, I'm looking for Chocolate Chip Clif Bars.

Now the guy at the counter says, "Oh, we're out of them."

The cop hears us. "Oh, energy, like protein, Clif Bars?" he asks.

"No, no, no." I shake my head. "I mean, when I have one, I only eat one." This is one of the most blatant lies I've ever uttered.

"Oh, well, we have other flavors," says the guy at the counter.

"No, no. I'm good. It was that one bar I wanted because my energy is low." I leave the store feeling like a total douche bag. But what do I do next? I walk to Whole Foods to see if they have Chocolate Chip Clif Bars. They do. I eat two.

Two or three more hours go by and I'm hungry again, and someone says, "There's food over at crafty." I go over to craft services and there's this whole Italian thing set up. There's meat lasagna—I prefer vegetable lasagna, but there's no vegetable, so I take a big chunk of meat lasagna. So big that I can't even put it on a plate; I have to put it in a bowl. I'm eating it, and I look up, and there's Officer-Fucking-Heart-Attack. I don't wait for his reaction. I take one forkful, and I say, "That's all I need," and toss it. I don't care if I recycle the bowl or not. I'm aghast. I did it for him, but I guess I benefited.

These retired cops should start a food security service for overeating actors. Every time you're about to take a bite of something bad at the craft service table, they appear out of the shadows and just stare at you. They'd make a fortune.

FRIDAY, MARCH 20, 2009

I didn't read my meditation today.

Today we're filming Larry up on the roof of the *Seinfeld* offices. I'm jonesing for tacos from my favorite taco place, Henry's Tacos. I'm thinking, *How can I get someone to go get me some tacos?* It's bad enough that I'm going to eat tacos, but I'm scheming for someone else to get them for me. What I do is mention tacos to someone in the crew, and soon enough the craving spreads. The crew all wants them. I tell Erin, "The crew wants Henry's Tacos." She tells me that she's already ordered a second meal for that night. One of the other producers hears this and says to Erin, "Why don't you order some tacos for the crew and we'll (meaning myself and a few other producers) pay for it." When the tacos arrive later in the night, my share comes to $170. I eat two tacos. Which I better have enjoyed. They cost me $85 apiece.

SUNDAY, MARCH 22, 2009
Weigh in . . .
Weight: 270
Blood Sugar: 128
Wii Fit age: 55

Everything is going up. No surprise. NURSING! (That's a favorite non sequitur of mine.) But if I don't change my ways, nursing is what I'll need.

MONDAY, MARCH 23, 2009
Today's meditation is about awareness. It tells me that to be aware is to be focused and alive. *If we are truly alert to what is going on within and around us, we will never be bored . . . but sometimes this new awareness brings pain.* If I'm eating, I'm not bored, but then again I'm not feeling anything in particular. Neither boredom nor pain.

We are filming at the golf course at Mountain Gate Country Club, and it's very, very windy. This is the scene where Larry kills a swan with his golf club.

Today's my son James's thirteenth birthday. So after school's out, my wife brings him to the set. As per usual when my children come to visit, they are most concerned with the craft service table. If you asked them about their memories of my time making movies and television shows, it would probably be about what candy they served at craft service.

We took my son out to dinner last night. For the last six years he's chosen Benihana. Even on years when I'm not watching what I eat, I get nauseous at Benihana. I'm not a big fan of people cooking at my table. Cook in the kitchen, bring it to me, I trust you know what you are doing. Even when I ask them to prepare it a certain way, without two pounds of butter, I get nauseous. I'm sick to my stomach just writing about Benihana. But it's for my son, so I do it.

Well, this year James wanted to go to the Brazilian place where they cut your meat in front of you, Fogo de Chao. That place makes me embarrassed. Men in costume come to your table with a giant slab of meat—essentially a cow—and a metal rod and knife, and slice it right into your plate, and you just keep eating and eating. Essentially you never have to stop.

As you know, I'm trying to become a vegetarian. Actually, I've been trying to be a vegetarian for about five years. But what do you do at a place like Fogo de Chao? It's not like they come over and say, "More salad? Can I slice this tomato for you?"

TUESDAY, MARCH 24, 2009
I seem to have misplaced my Food for Thought meditation book. I also can't find my wallet or my iPhone. Welcome to the world of ADD.

I'm going to be filming with some of my closest friends today. Besides Larry, there's Paul Mazursky as Norm, Greg Pritikin as

Norm's friend Jimbo, Bob Einstein as Marty Funkhauser, and Richard Kind as Larry's cousin Andy. I love them all. Here's what's funny: you're crazy lucky to be working with your friends, but then my friends (actually, just Kind and Einstein— they're nuts) end up driving me crazy. Also, put a bunch of friends together on a set, and you get a lot of juvenile behavior from adults, often instigated by me.

Meanwhile, I've gone crazy for Clif Bars. Chocolate Chip Clif Bars. Fuck you, Zeke. Craft services ordered me a box of Clif Bars, and I bet you I ate three-fourths of a box. That's got to be fifteen Clif Bars in two days.

WEDNESDAY, MARCH 25, 2009

Today was a typical day for me, typical of my behavior in previous years, now that I've starting eating badly again. (You've noticed that I'm eating badly again, haven't you?) Here's how it goes. I start the day with promise and excitement. I really am taking care of myself. I follow through until sometime in the afternoon, and then I drift toward craft services, where Pop-Tarts and Fruity Pebbles beckon. Who needs a Clif Bar? And once I've eaten the Pop-Tarts and Fruity Pebbles, I think, *When they pull out pizza later, will I have some of that?* Then I go home and go to bed, but I have tons of anxiety, so I don't fall asleep until three in the morning. The next morning I wake up really happy.

It's the same cycle, over and over and over again, fueled by the following justification: *I'm eating these Fruity Pebbles, and we're filming this really funny scene, and I'll always remember, when I see this scene, that that was the day I got sober.* Each time is always going to be the last time.

The thing is, I could write a history of *Curb Your Enthusiasm* through my food consumption. Name a scene. How about the big vagina scene, where I'm sitting with Larry by the hospital bed? That was filmed in Pasadena, and I ate a bunch of ribs, and then I said, that'll be it. I'll remember the big vagina scene, because that will be the last time I ate beef. That will be funny; I can talk about big vaginas whenever I tell people I'm a vegetarian. Now raise your hand if you think I ate meat for the last time after the big vagina scene?

How about when I told Larry that Cheryl popped into my mind when I was fantasizing about Jenna Jameson? That day I had some Twizzlers. I was great with my eating all day, and then I remembered that they were on the cart. Generally they only have red vines, but the craft service people said, "I know you love Twizzlers," and they got Twizzlers for me. (You can think of the craft service people as my enablers.) Could I really say, "No, I'm not supposed to have sugar?" So I ate Twizzlers on the day I told Larry that I wacked off to Cheryl.

How about the scene where Larry and I are watching *Girls Gone Wild* and my dog runs away? Every break we had I went out to the craft service table and had an egg salad sandwich. I bet I had at least six that afternoon. Yes, I got sick. And, no, I'm not usually a freak for egg salad.

Every day I think it's going to be different, and every day is the same. And then the dread descends at night, and I can't sleep. But something fantastic happened last night. I actually woke my wife up and we talked about it, and I went back to sleep. Take it from a married man, the last person you think you can count on to calm you down is your wife. And she shocked the shit out of me; she put me at ease. I love her every day, but I love her even more now. Actually, that's not true. I tell her all the time that I couldn't love her more even if I tried. Getting old sucks, but it's nice to grow old with someone.

MONDAY, MARCH 30, 2009

Today is the worst day of filming of the whole season, in the most beautiful place in L.A. We're at Westward Beach in Malibu. Later I find out it's where they filmed the end of the movie *Planet of the Apes*, and I call Dave Mandel (one of the producers of *Curb*), the only other comic-book geek on the set who would know this fact or care, and he says, "Of course I knew."

Anyway, we're shooting a scene in which my daughter almost drowns because of Larry and his BlackBerry. I still haven't found my book of meditations. But, for some reason, today I have found great resolve to return to healthy eating.

I have to go in the ocean today, and I'm a little nervous about it. I'm an excellent swimmer; it's just that the water is mighty cold. They've fitted me for a wet suit to wear under my clothes. In the late afternoon Karie (the sweet P.A. who I snapped at a few weeks ago) comes to my trailer to get me.

"Okay, we're ready," she says.

"No one told me to get ready."

I need help getting the wet suit on. I let her know that I

need a few minutes and I try to put it on myself. I take off my clothes and manage to get the wet suit halfway on, when she comes back two minutes later and says to relax, I'm not needed yet. I peel the suit off my legs and sit down in my underwear.

Another two minutes and she comes back, "Ready on set." Thank God Christina the costumer arrives to help me with the wet suit. I head to set, and we rehearse. I go back to my trailer, and Karie helps me shower. It isn't what it sounds like. I just have to make sure that my hair and clothes are wet. I go back to the set. Not ready at set. The poor actress playing my daughter, Ashly Holloway, is not wearing a wet suit. She's wearing a bathing suit and she's freezing. This is much worse for her.

At last they're ready and we head into the ocean. There's a big undertow and I'm getting slammed by the waves. I'm holding Ashly and blocking the waves. I help carry her out of the ocean. Susie screams at Larry. We do this over and over, and over and over. Then there is some sort of problem and we wait fifteen minutes, me in my wet suit, Ashly in her bathing suit. I'm concerned for Ashly. She's shaking. Now I'm angry. A few more takes and we get it. When we're done, I realize that someone has taken my towel. The annoying thing about all this is that it will end up only being seconds of screen time.

As I'm driving home, I decide to go to Brent's Deli, the best deli in L.A., as far as I'm concerned. As I'm pulling in, I say to myself, "Nothing good can come of this." Yet I go in anyway and order a Reuben. Strangely enough, I've never had a Reuben sandwich in my whole life. When it comes, I wish I had ordered it years ago. Because my tastes have changed. It's too salty for me now. I only take a few bites. As I eat the potato pancake that comes on the side, I can't help but notice an old woman coughing loudly at the next table. No matter how much she coughs, her husband never stops eating. Hunger is a powerful thing. Poor woman; she could die and he wouldn't notice.

The waiter comes over to me. "You done?"

"I'm full."

He looks at my sandwich with only a couple of bites missing.

"What happened, you don't like it?"

"I like it a lot. I just can't eat that much."

He takes it away.

I'm not saying I'm a hero here or anything, but it's a small triumph that I didn't eat that sandwich.

15

A short nap can refresh us much more than unnecessary food; a period of meditation can lift us out of mental and emotional depression. Obviously, I found my meditation book. And speaking of meditation, Jerry Seinfeld told me about Transcendental Meditation. I've been searching for something to help bring me a sense of peace and reduce my anxiety.

We are filming a scene at Larry David's house in Brentwood, where Larry offers to put his cousin Andy's daughter through college. Today is the day I finally start my monthlong, only-taking-the-bus festival. I have to leave at 7:20 a.m. to make a 9:00 a.m. call time. Nonetheless, I left my house this morning so crazy excited. I don't like walking unless I have a destination, so I was happy to be bouncing to the bus. My wife was so proud of me as I walked out the door—and she also thought I was an idiot. I think that she is both proud and thinks I'm an idiot every day, but today the dichotomy is heightened. She actually offered me a ride to the bus stop. Very nice of her, but I don't think she's quite getting it.

As I'm walking down the hill (a steep hill), I pass a neighbor walking his dog, and I say to him, "I'm taking the bus today," as if I'm an eight-year-old on his first day of school.

"Oh, good for you. That's great, that's great."

Now, it's about a mile walk from my house to the bus stop. About midway, there's a busy street with no sidewalk, so there's a level of danger, which today only adds to the excitement. I pass by my old house, which isn't far from where I live now. I used to live down the block from this Jewish guy who actually built his own fence. I remember being so impressed that a Jew would build a fence. I'd see him working on it and think, *What are you doing?* Not only did he physically not look like the type of guy to build a fence, but it seemed so out of character. I am not Baron von Religious, but I follow the credo of Jews throughout history—which is, *I have an idea to build a fence; hey, I'll pay somebody to build my fence. Whatever the price, I'll be happy to pay it. I'll pay them, and I'll probably serve them lunch.* But this Jew actually built his own fence. As I pass by it on my way to the bus stop, I notice that flowers and vines have grown all over it. And it occurs to me that I have driven by that fence many times in the years since I lived here and never once noticed the flowering vines. Just as healthy eating retrained my taste buds to appreciate a low-sodium diet, maybe this walking business will teach me to appreciate nature without Blu-ray.

When I get to the bus stop, there are about forty people waiting—at seven-forty-five in the morning. I take out my iPhone to call my wife and tell her that I made it. She was a bit nervous because of the part of the walk where there is no sidewalk and the trucks come flying by. Remember that I had considered getting a bicycle to ride to the bus, after Ed told me that you can put your bike on the front. But my family voted that I'm not allowed to ride a bike to the bus. Or for that matter, anywhere in the city. They think I'll hurt myself.

So I call my wife, and while I'm talking to her, I realize that nobody around me has an iPhone. In fact, there is not one person at this bus stop who wouldn't be driving if they had a car. I'm certainly the only idiot doing it for my carbon footprint, and I worry that I'm calling attention to myself by talking on my iPhone, so I end the call quickly and put it away. If I'm going to be taking the bus with these people for the next month, I don't want them thinking that the new guy with the iPhone's a douche bag.

At this point, the bus pulls up, and all these people get on. I'm talking about every single one of them. Which makes me nervous because I don't think it's the right number bus for me, and as a matter of pride, I'm not going to ask anyone. I want to do it myself. As the doors close, I'm standing there alone, anxiously wondering if I missed my bus, when another one with the right number pulls up. I get on and show my pass— this is all very exciting.

Now, I had thought that taking the bus would be relaxing, that I would read or perhaps pull out my notebook, jot down some notes. I have a long ride until I have to change buses, plenty of time to relax. Turns out, it is packed, hugely packed. There is no place to sit. I stand for about ten minutes until someone gets off right behind me and I can finally sit down.

But the only available seat is a priority seat for someone who's older, handicapped, or pregnant. So from that moment on I'm sitting there stressed, thinking, *If somebody old or pregnant or wheelchair-bound gets on, I'm screwed.* I peer out the windows as we approach each stop, praying that everyone waiting is young, male, and healthy.

Meanwhile, I'm sitting across from a woman who looks like an angry librarian, and she's staring at me with the greatest disdain. I wonder if she's thinking, *Why are you here? You have a car. Why are you on the bus? What are you trying to prove? I have to be here. What's your excuse?* She keeps clearing her throat, and I'm convinced that she's waiting for me to take the hint and relinquish my priority seat. But I'm terrified of having to stand again. I have a horrible back and the sure way to aggravate it is to stand for long periods of time. I would be a miserable salesclerk. I'm tempted to say to the lady, "Look, I need to sit. My back is bad." But I don't dare speak, nor do I feel I can do anything else.

I don't know why I'm feeling so intimidated, but for whatever reason, I'm afraid to do anything. It's a little hot on the bus, but I'm afraid to take off my jacket. I don't want to pull out my iPhone and listen to songs. I just want to remain as innocuous as possible. I'm afraid to fall asleep. There's no music, no talking—the bus is completely silent. You can hear everyone breathing.

Toward the end of the ride a woman gets on. Under normal circumstances, I would get up for a woman. But not today. At least she's young, probably in her thirties. After all the anticipation, it's an awkward, long bus ride.

I'm waiting in Westwood for my second bus, again worried about catching the right one. Two buses show up, and whoosh, fifty people get on, same as this morning. Behind them, my bus, "Santa Monica 3," pulls up. There it is. I'm walking up to the door and boom, it pulls off. What! People inside stare at me blankly as the driver takes off.

Bus drivers never make eye contact. That must be the first rule of bus driving school: if someone's running to the bus, don't make eye contact. Don't let them know you see them.

Ten to fifteen more minutes go by, and a couple of buses pull up at the same time. I watch as a girl gets off the second bus and runs to catch the first one. But the bus driver closes the door on her and takes off. Then my bus comes around and it doesn't even hesitate long enough to stop.

This girl is furious, I'm furious, we're both furious together. What the fuck! The bus driver who originally dropped her off saw the whole thing and actually yells out, "You should report it." I take out my space pen and a notepad and write down the number to call with complaints. My first bus day and I'm making complaints. After another five minutes the girl gets her bus, but ten minutes pass and mine still is not coming. I am tempted to call a producer of *Curb* and have them send a van to pick me up, but I think *no*. No matter how late I get there, I have to stick with my mission. I decide to walk down to the corner—there is another stop there. I look up at the sign and see my bus number. I wasn't standing at the right stop. I laugh.

Finally, I get on the bus to Brentwood. I realize that my whole commute today, a commute that would normally take me, with traffic, maybe forty minutes, takes me two and a half hours. The bus drops me off about a half mile away from the set, and one of the transportation guys on *Curb Your Enthusiasm* sees me walking and is clearly confused.

"I left the space open for you. You didn't have to park over there." He's referring to my usual parking space by my trailer, thinking that I'm walking from where I've parked my car.

"No. I took the bus."

"Oh . . ." he says, not sure what to make of this information. He considers me for a moment and then adds helpfully, "I took a train once."

When I finally get to the set everybody is so impressed. They really feel like I have accomplished something. Some people travel that far by bus every day for work. I am so lucky to have a car.

FRIDAY, APRIL 3, 2009
I'm late for the bus; I don't have time to read my meditation.

I came up with a rule that I can ride in a car, but only if I'm going somewhere that is on somebody's way exactly. Like, you couldn't even go a block out of your way to drop me off. That was my rule.

After filming that first day of riding the bus, Richard Kind has to go right past my house on his way to his place, so I let him drop me off at my home. Another day last week, my wife was going somewhere that would help me get closer to work, so she dropped me off at the bus stop that was right on the way.

The bus moves along and is making its stops, and suddenly at one of the stops, there's a pounding on the window and I hear, "That's Jeff Garlin! That's Jeff Garlin!"

It was my wife. She was in front of the Starbucks where the bus stopped. She saw me coming and couldn't resist. By the way, in the last two weeks of taking the bus, I've never been recognized. I'm thinking there's not one person who has HBO who rides the bus.

Sometimes the bus is really hot, sometimes really crowded, sometimes both. Usually you see "regulars." There's a guy in a shiny Cubs jacket, but the shine has faded away, so he has that one-step-from-homelessness look about him. There's a man in a wheelchair I see a lot, and every time I do I think, *This guy is in his fucking wheelchair and he's taking the bus constantly. What am I even remotely complaining about?*

SATURDAY, APRIL 4, 2009

Let me give you an example of the sort of everyday thing that can happen to derail my efforts at eating well. Last night I went to see Denis Leary's show at L.A. Live with Marla and James. He hosted a show featuring comedians that are on his television show. At some point during the show I went to the lobby. I said to two lady ushers in red vests, "Where are the water fountains?"

"We don't have any."

"You don't have any public water fountains?"

"They're upstairs on the mezzanine."

"Great."

"Oh, but the upstairs is closed tonight."

"How do I get some water?"

They both looked confused. Then as if a lightbulb went off, one of them said, "If you go to the snack bar, they'll give you a cup of water."

At the snack bar I get in a line of about ten people. A guy, I assume it's the manager, comes out from behind the snack bar, points at me, and says, "You're the last in the line! We're not serving anyone past you."

He says it in a way that makes me think I'm supposed to inform others that come up in line behind me. So I say to the first guy who comes up, "I'm sorry, they are not serving anyone else past me. That is what they just said to me, but I don't like this responsibility, so if you choose to stay it's your business, but I thought I'd inform you. If a line forms behind you I'm not telling anyone else; I don't want to be involved."

Other people in line nod, saying, yeah, it shouldn't be your responsibility. Then after about ten minutes I'm in the front of the line. To have to wait in line for a drink of water out of a plastic cup is ridiculous, not to mention wasteful.

"May I have some water please?"

"Four dollars."

"Not bottled water. A cup of water."

"We don't have cups of water."

"I was told I could get a cup of water at the snack bar."

"Where did you hear that?"

"One of the ladies in the red vests told me to go to the snack bar for some water."

"She meant bottled water."

"No, she meant a cup of water."

"How do you know what she meant?"

"Because I heard her."

"If you want water, there are fountains up on the mezzanine."

"The mezzanine is closed. That's why she told me to go to the snack bar. She said you would give me some water."

"She is security; she has no authority."

I didn't know you needed authority to help someone get a drink of water. "Well, don't you have water?"

"No, we don't."

"What about that soda dispenser?"

"Do you want a Coke?"

"No. I want water." It would have been so much easier to buy a bottled water than to have this insane conversation. But I can't give up now.

"I told you, we don't have any water except bottled water."

"I know that soda dispenser has water."

"It doesn't."

"Yes. It does."

"How do you know it does?"

"Everyone knows. I've used them at McDonald's."

"Well, this isn't McDonald's."

He's lying. All of those dispensers have water. And if it's not regular water, then it's seltzer water, but there is water.

"May I please have some water?"

Finally he says, "Well, we have the sink right here."

I tell him to give me water from the sink, as if I'm a daredevil. He gives me the water from the sink, but he doesn't let it run. He gives me the first water that comes out. I'm fuming.

"You know what, forget it."

"You don't want this water?"

"You win. Give me three bottled waters."

"Twelve dollars." He grabs the waters out of a minifridge behind him.

"I'll have a hot dog, too. Make that two."

SUNDAY, APRIL 5, 2009

Weight: 271

Blood Sugar: 134

I've stopped with the Wii Fit. It doesn't know how old I am. CORN.

MONDAY, APRIL 6, 2009

I think I have pinkeye. My wife is sure I caught it on the bus. She is also convinced that I will get swine flu on the bus, and is pressuring me to stop taking it. The one thing I will admit is that I'm not going many places. Now that I'm taking the bus everywhere, I've made transportation an as-needed situation. No going anywhere for fun.

SATURDAY, APRIL 11, 2009

I drove tonight. We went out with some friends and my wife had a couple glasses of wine, which she never does, so she was, for her, drunk. And I had to drive home. And I have to say, it felt quite good.

MONDAY, APRIL 13, 2009

I've officially stopped taking the bus. It's like a diet—you can follow it perfectly for months, and then you eat one thing you're not supposed to, just one thing, and it's all off. So the bus riding lasted for two weeks. And the reason I stopped was because my wife was driving the kids to school every day, picking them up, taking them here, taking them there, and doing all the errands. There was nothing that I was contributing to the house. At first she was really supportive, but as time went on, she wasn't thrilled with me, to say the least. Being green isn't always convenient. I guess that's part of the reason this country has gotten into this situation with the environment. Also, today is Marla's birthday, so she wins.

WEDNESDAY, APRIL 15, 2009

I had this idea that I would choose a random day and record everything that happened as if I were a reporter. I hope it's interesting.

This is it.

6:20 a.m. Wake up.

6:25 a.m. Read *Chicago Tribune* online.

6:45 a.m. Wake up family.

7:00 a.m. Cardio for twenty-five minutes while watching *The Soup*.

7:55 a.m. Take Duke to school.

8:30 a.m. Arrive at work.

9:00 a.m. Have seizure.

By the way, I get complex partial seizures. The technical definition is an epileptic seizure that causes impairment of awareness or responsiveness. It always starts with a feeling of déjà vu and a sort of impending doom. Then I get racing thoughts that contain scenes from dreams I've had. It also makes my vision kind of blurry. When I first got them, they were quite scary. In my twenties, I always thought they were anxiety attacks, as a way for my subconscious mind to release tension. If you saw me having one, you couldn't tell I was having a seizure.

I call Erin (my confidante and producer) over and tell her I'm having a seizure. She's confused, so I explain the best I can while having a seizure. She holds my hand and talks me through it.

10:00 a.m. Shooting a scene with Cheryl and Larry. I watch the take and give a few notes.

1:45 p.m. Go home and take nap.

3:45 p.m. Realize I can't sleep and go downstairs to let my barking dogs out. I turn and see my son's friend. I'm standing in my underwear, embarrassed and bloated. I say hello. I hear another, "Hello, Mr. Garlin." It's my son's friend's nanny saying hello. Embarrassed and still bloated, I say hello, then go get dressed.

5:15 p.m. Arrive back at work at the Radford lot. I run into my friend Tim and have dinner with him. Coconut rice with broccoli. We film some more; I have fewer notes this time. I eat some sushi and leave.

7:00 p.m. Arrive at the Motion Picture Academy for an screening of Fellini's 8½. I see Alexander Payne. I met him once at an awards function, and after that he watched an early cut of my movie, *I Want Someone to Eat Cheese With*, and gave me some notes. Very kind and very generous. I haven't seen him since and I wanted to thank him again. I introduce myself again and say a very quick hello. Before I can thank him and tell him what happened with my movie, some friends of his arrive, and he turns to me and says "Thanks for saying hello."

What does that mean? Who thanks someone for saying hello? I guess it means *I don't remember you and please walk away from me now*. I feel pretty stupid. I go into the theater, sit in the last row, and chat with the ushers.

The program begins, and the head of UCLA's film school speaks about Fellini. I watch the film. I want to look like Mastroianni in his suits. I leave and look in the mirror on the way out: fat. The Beatles' "Carry That Weight" is playing in my car.

9:00 p.m. Get home. Pay babysitter. Eat cold pizza. Take my meds. Go to bed.

SUNDAY, APRIL 19, 2009
Weight: 273
Blood Sugar: 148
It's all going to pot. DUTCH APPLE.

We're finally having our bathroom redone. They tore it apart on Wednesday and Thursday, so we're pretty much living on the first floor. We go upstairs to my son's room sometimes, but mostly we keep to the main floor. I'm not feeling great, so I tell my wife that I'm just going to hang out in our basement and watch movies, or watch the Cubs if they're on. I need to relax. Just as I'm leaning back in my chair, my brother-in-law, who stopped by for a visit, comes downstairs and announces, "You have asbestos in your bathroom."

"Are you kidding me?" I go upstairs to the bathroom, and he's right, there's asbestos on the air-conditioning vent. It's on a vent. By the way, asbestos looks like surgical tape that's been wrapped around a pipe or a vent. It's Friday afternoon and the workers are gone. Immediately I'm wondering, did they know there was asbestos? I call up the contractor, who tells me, "Yeah, we're pretty sure it is asbestos."

"Why didn't you let anyone know?" I ask.

"I didn't want to scare you," he says.

"Didn't want to scare me? I'm an adult and I need to know if there's asbestos in my bathroom, especially with two children running around." And not only that, but the air conditioner is running, and the top of the vent is a little bit messy, so it's basically blowing asbestos around the room. "How could you not tell me?" I ask.

"My bad," he says. Which only makes me angrier because I have a whole thing against "my bad." In my opinion, "my bad" came from someone, somewhere, who heard it while working with mentally challenged people, and brought it out into the mainstream. Whatever happened to, "I'm terribly sorry, I've made a mistake"? You don't follow, "I didn't tell you about the asbestos in your upstairs bathroom" with "My bad."

I'm pretty furious. I don't slam the phone down on the guy, but I say, "I'm really angry about this," and hang up. At this point I'm also really angry at my wife because, as you know, this contractor was somebody that she found. I wanted her to work with Ron and Tammy at REAS, to get a checklist, or at least have the contractor talk to Tammy to make sure they're on the same page. Because one of the things I'm doing to make my house more green is putting new insulation in, as Ron and Tammy suggested. When the workers, who I'd hired through REAS, were installing it, they found some asbestos. They came right down, they told me, and the next day it was removed. That's what it's like working with REAS; they know what they're doing.

Let me remind you that instead of talking to REAS, my wife asked the contractor—the guy I was just talking to, the one who said, "my bad" if he was green, and he said, "Yes, I've done lots of green work." What do you think that means?

I call the guy back and I say, "Hey, man, I just wanted to let you know I don't understand. I think it's crazy that you didn't tell me. I've got kids in the house. It's an air-conditioning vent. The air-conditioning is running. Why wouldn't you tell me this?"

"I'm terribly sorry," he says. "It was a stupid mistake." He says he's going to bring his guy on Monday. But I don't know. You have to be licensed to remove asbestos.

After I get off the phone, my wife's cousin, who does a lot of rebuilding on his own, has come over, and I ask him to please come upstairs and take a look at the bathroom. I'm a little worried that he doesn't really know what he's doing, at least when it concerns toxic chemicals. What gives me a clue is that he's touching and rubbing the asbestos.

"Should you be doing that?"

"It's fine."

"No, it's not fine."

"I'll wash my hands." Which he does. But Lord knows, he was putting it in the air and he was even smelling it. I don't think it was enough exposure to kill him, or anyone. But what is going on here? I'm trying to make my house ecologically sound, and now my entire family might be breathing asbestos all weekend.

SATURDAY, APRIL 25, 2009

I barely slept last night, after what happened yesterday. Today Ron from REAS comes over, and we talk to the air-conditioner guy and the removal people. And he's hooking me up with the green contractor, which my wife, at this point, really can't fight me on. In the end, the asbestos might help me win a lot of battles. Although I'm still not sure I'll get the double-pane windows. I'm coming to realize that I need to be content with small victories—you can't save the world, or yourself, in a few days or months.

TUESDAY, APRIL 28, 2009

We're filming at CBS Radford again, a scene where Larry and Jerry discuss their assistant's attire. I tell Charlie in craft services not to order any more Clif Bars. I say, "I don't care if you have them for the set, but please, none for me. And if you see me eating a Clif Bar, I will give you a thousand dollars." He starts putting Clif Bars everywhere, in my dressing room, on the set. Then I start giving Clif Bars to members of the crew, and I tell them to leave the wrappers for him to find. He's getting very suspicious. I do actually eat a Clif Bar today. Trader Joe's is a block away, and I walk over to buy a Clif Bar, while we're filming something, too—that's how bad it gets. I get a jones, and I have to go get it.

WEDNESDAY, APRIL 29, 2009

I haven't taken the bus for a couple of weeks, but I see on the news that yesterday the police caught a murderer on a bus. In Beverlywood on Pico, they pulled a bus over, and people were getting off the bus with their hands behind their heads, one after another until they got the murderer. He didn't commit murder on the bus, but he was riding it when he got busted. I said to myself, *I'm never taking the bus again.* But then last night I was at an event for the National Resources Defense Council, the NRDC, and I ran into Ed Begley. (I also saw a lot of eight-cylinders in the parking lot. You're at an NRDC event, and a BMW 750 pulls up! It's crazy.) Ed told me how proud he was of me that I was taking the bus. I was honest and told him that I'd stopped for now. He's still impressed that I did it at all. I told him that I planned to still occasionally take the bus.

But I have to say the bus does suck here. I'm telling *you* this, not Ed. If you have to take the bus, I'm sorry. The bus in L.A. is horrible. It's unsettling. It's nauseating. And there are murderers! Who wants to ride the bus with murderers? Not me. Now, that would be something that would help me sell my book—if I had been one of the people on that bus with the murderer, and there's a chance I could have been since we were filming on Pico, even though nobody got hurt and everything worked out in the end. In any case, I'm not sure if I'll take the bus anymore.

Did I mention that I know a guy who takes the bus everywhere? A very successful guy. He told me he even takes the bus to strip clubs with a thousand dollars in his pocket. Murderers and degenerates, I tell you.

SUNDAY, MAY 3, 2009
Weight: 274
Blood Sugar: 152
What can I say? GAZEBO.

MONDAY, MAY 4, 2009
Food for Thought—"*Food Is Not Enough*": "*Food is fine, as far as it goes, but it doesn't go far enough. We need our three meals a day,*

planned according to the requirements for healthy nutrition, but we do not live by food alone. We need close contacts with friends. We need to be involved in productive work and stimulating activities. We need to serve in the areas where we are best qualified. We need to use our God-given talents and abilities rather than sitting on them." Today I'm quoting the book exactly as is. No interpretations. As much as I've enjoyed my meditations, I clearly haven't taken them very seriously. The above meditation hits me hard. I keep reading it all day.

It's the last day of filming at my house in the Pacific Palisades. Larry comes over and accuses Susie of having ruined Julia's table. After a number of takes where I've been sitting, I get up, and Jonas, our key grip, asks me if I'm all right. I think back to what Jessica said about me being the evolution of man as I get up. At lunch I eat a ton. All out of habit. I have to get out of this rut.

WEDNESDAY, MAY 6, 2009

Food for Thought—"Communicating": "If we do not tell people what is troubling us, they cannot help. We have sometimes been too proud or too shy to let others know what we were feeling. Rather than trying to communicate with those close to us, we ate. Eating instead of communicating further increased our isolation and unhappiness. Exposing our feelings makes us vulnerable, and we often fear that we will be hurt or rejected. We may be trying to preserve a false image of ourselves as self-sufficient and free of problems.

Whatever the reasons for our unwillingness to communicate, we are cheating ourselves. By 'clamming up,' we cut ourselves off from the care and support of those who love us."

Verbatim again.

We are shooting at what was supposed to be Jerry Seinfeld's backyard. I'm really getting depressed because I haven't lost enough weight and the end of filming is only a day away. I spend most of the day alone, listening to my iPod.

THURSDAY, MAY 7, 2009

Today's meditation is about how *when angry, many of us overeat.*

It's the last day of filming on Season 7. Which means that today is my assistant's last day. Obviously, I didn't fire her. Obviously, I'm happy about that. I don't want to say anymore because I don't want to be sarcastic.

It's amazing to think that *Curb's* been on the air for seven seasons. You have to understand that in the beginning the intention was never to have a hit TV series. We made an hour-long HBO special. A onetime thing. I told you about that first day of filming when Larry said to me, "Wouldn't it be great to do this as a series?"

I remember it so clearly. But I also forgot it instantly. I never thought it would happen. When we shot the first season, we did what we thought was funny, thinking that there was no way anyone else would think it was funny. But to my amazement, they did. So know that I'm grateful to have this success.

Today we are filming Jason's book party at Julia's house. It's rather hot outside, but I manage to find a nice, quiet, air-conditioned room. I close my eyes and relax. Even though I've been on the sidelines a bit this year, today, the last day of filming, it's with a tear in my eye that drops into the hand of a little girl who catches it and looks up and says to me, "Why so sad, mister?"

"I don't know. Not happy in my work I guess."

"Why is that?"

"Well, since you asked, sometimes I wish that I . . ."

Jerry walks over.

"What's going on?"

The strange little girl tells him, "Jeff's sad. I don't think he gets enough satisfaction with his work. I also think he feels old and that he hasn't accomplished enough."

"I never said that."

Jerry then puts his arm around me and says, "I really can't associate with any of that. I look much younger than my age and I'm immensely successful."

Michael, Julia, and Jason walk over.

Jerry tells them, "Jeff is jealous of my success and good looks."

"I never said that!"

Then the four of them hug and tell me it will all be okay. Larry comes over. "Why are you hugging him?" he asks.

Julia looks at Larry angrily and says, "Because you won't."

I shout, "I never said that!"

Larry replies, "I know you didn't, Jeff. You're just day-dreaming all of this."

Susie and Cheryl walk over. And Susie says, "Is he creating another one of those fucking stupid scenarios in his imagination again?"

Then the little girl looks up at me and says, "Ignore her. I'm real. And because I caught your teardrop, you can have any wish you want. There is only one caveat. It can't include the word 'lotion.' "

I bend down and whisper my wish in her ear and she replies, "That's it, that's all you want?"

"That's it."

"Done."

"Thank you."

"My pleasure. I'm going to leave now."

"Bye."

And with that she flies off and we all wave good-bye to her.

Larry says, "I liked that little girl. I really did. I'm going to miss her. She really affected me. You know what? I'm going to rename my production company Rainbow and Lollipops Productions. And in honor of that, for lunch today I'm going to serve up some fresh grilled rainbows and lollipops."

Then Susie says, "I'm never going to swear again."

By the way, if I tell you what I wished for, it won't happen.

• • •

Okay, so we didn't have rainbows and lollipops for lunch. Actually, on the last day of filming they always serve all kinds of great food. Steak and sushi and all sorts of good stuff, and I have a little bit of everything from every little world they created as if I'm back at Disneyland. I think, *Okay, I'll start fresh tomorrow.*

16

Tomorrow is now. I've got to change things. How's this for action? Tonight I leave for Pritikin. Things have gotten out of control. I figure another week there and I'll be focused. Focused and feeling good.

FRIDAY, MAY 15, 2009

I'm in Dr. Bauer's office. I've been at Pritikin for a week and I'm feeling great.

"You're a changed man," he says.

I agree with him, but I ask, "How so?"

"First of all, you came in weighing the same as when you last left in January. That's great progress. Most people come back having gained weight."

I don't tell him that when I got home from Pritikin in January, I lost eight more pounds. Then put it back on. If I waited another couple of weeks to come back here, I would have surely gained more weight.

"Also, you've stayed off the road. You've put your health and family before the glow of the spotlight."

Okay, a couple of thoughts here. Know that performing stand-up on the road, which until last summer I did all the time, was torturous to my body. My typical schedule was: arrive in a city Thursday night, wake up before dawn on Friday to do press until about noon, then two shows Friday night, wake up early again on Saturday (just because that's what my body clock tells me. I'm not in any town long enough to get acclimated. Also, I have a tough time sleeping away from my family). Two more shows on Saturday night, leave at the crack of dawn on Sunday to go back home. I would try to eat right. Good luck to me on that one. And I would exercise maybe once. But it wasn't enough. I did this schedule with varying changes for more than twenty-five years. The doctor thinks I did this for the "glow of the spotlight." But it's what I do for a living. What I've always done since I was twenty years old. I am passionate about it, but I think the doctor has the wrong idea. For me, it's not about the glow of the spotlight, it's just what I do. Nevertheless, I haven't done comedy on the road since last summer. I knew it was a barrier to getting healthy.

But hopefully he's right about me being a changed man.

SATURDAY, MAY 16, 2009

For a while, I've been thinking about trying Transcendental Meditation. TM. Last month, Jerry Seinfeld told me about how wonderful it's been for him. And, most recently, a lovely woman named Maria raved about it while I was at Pritikin. I first discovered it by reading David Lynch's book, *Catching the Big Fish*. He writes that it's not about religion, it's not about God. It's about being at peace with yourself and the world. Twice a day you meditate, and you function better. And it's good for your health. There is all kinds of scientific proof.

Today is my first meeting at the TM Center in Beverly Hills. It's actually a small house off Wilshire Boulevard. When I arrive, I'm greeted by a woman dressed in business attire, like an executive secretary. She asks me to take my shoes off when I come in. She's very kind and welcoming. "How are you? Come right in." There's also a heavy gentleman in a tight-fitting beige suit, with a white shirt and a multicolor pastel tie. "Hello, uh, how are you? Please sit down," he says.

This is their conversation for the first ten minutes I'm sitting there:

"Oh boy, we need some seats."

"We need to get some more seats. Uh, Gloria, should we get Jim to get more seats?"

"We need more seats!"

At the time there were two or three people there, including me, and I think they are crazy. But soon at least fifteen people show up, making the leaders even more frantic.

"I'll tell you something, if we don't get some more seats, this could be chaotic."

"Are there any in the back?"

They seem like they're on the verge of yelling at one another. This isn't exactly a calming environment. Finally they start to give their presentation, and they're using a dry-erase board. Now, in all the excitement about the seats, they asked me to move to a spot where I'm the only person in the room who can't see the board. I can't see what they're doing; I just see occasional drawings for two seconds at a time. So, just listening to her voice, I'm falling asleep. I fall asleep numerous times, and keep on having to wake myself up. And all I'm thinking is, *Don't snore. There's a room full of people, don't snore.* To my knowledge, I didn't snore—but can the napper himself ever be sure?

They also give out pamphlets with scientific information. After my nap, I look through one, and I see that Russell Simmons is one of their poster boys. Now, who associates Russell Simmons with inner peace on any level? Here's what I think: *Successful entrepreneur. Record producer. Fashion. Nutty ex-wife.* I can't think of any associations that would be positive for this organization. In fact, I think about how much I hated *Def Comedy Jam* and how some smart comedians that I knew back in New York who were ruined artistically by that show. It made me tense, seeing Russell Simmons on that pamphlet. Although maybe TM made him realize he should get a divorce.

I'm fully awake now and the gentleman with the tie says something that captures my attention, "Once you go under, it is delicious." He said delicious. I love it. And then he kicks it up a notch. "I'll tell you something. When you come out, it is scrumptious." Fucking scrumptious. You know, I'm trying to avoid food to begin with and I associate "delicious" and "scrumptious" with food—actually, with Willy Wonka, to be precise. The thought that I can experience something that's

both delicious and scrumptious without food is very scrumpdil-
lyicious. No more living like an Augustus Gloop. I'm sold.

FRIDAY, MAY 22, 2009
Here's another conversation with my wife, as a way to give you
a sense of where we are in the greening of our house.

MARLA: You know how sometimes I get mad at you
when you put your green hat on and I call you green-
schmean? I have to say I've been resenting you a little
with this bathroom thing, because I do think it's green-
schmean.

JEFF: Why? The air quality's improving.

MARLA: Okay, fine, so we have to have our soy-based glue to
hold together the wood in our cabinets. Yes, those are all little things that count, and it all adds up. You have to work toward leading a green life.

JEFF: And it can be expensive.

MARLA: It is. But I'm not changing all the windows. You can
kiss my ass on that one.

JEFF: No, let's talk about that one.

MARLA: It's not going to happen. You can talk all you want.

JEFF: So it's never going to happen?

MARLA: Never.

JEFF: And it has only to do with the expense?

MARLA: I like my steel-case windows. And structurally, they hold up the house.

JEFF: Just know that we are going to do the windows at some point. It's not if, it's when.

MARLA: Okay, you can do that with your second wife. We're done. You've spent your money, we're moving on.

JEFF: It'll make the house quieter . . .

MARLA: Did you do this whole book project so you could get new windows?

JEFF: I didn't do a whole book so I could get new windows. I want new windows. It's a huge thing.

MARLA: Good for you. You'll get them next year . . .

JEFF: I will get them next year.

MARLA: . . . when you get your next wife.

———

JEFF: Are you leaving me?

MARLA: No, I'm not leaving you.

TUESDAY, MAY 26, 2009

Today I've agreed to be a guest on the new *Tonight* show. Not a real taping. A test show. But the reason I'm telling you about this has nothing to do with the show. It has to do with my dressing room. Or more specifically what is in my dressing room. Cupcakes. At least a dozen cupcakes. Great cupcakes. I know they are great not from eating them, but because there is a card lying next to them that says they're from Sprinkles Cupcakes in Beverly Hills. Many a time I have waited in line for cupcakes (always plural) at Sprinkles. But today I see them and it isn't even a possibility that I will have one. I don't even take them home. As far as I'm concerned, they're none of my business.

If you would've told me when I was waiting in line at Sprinkles one of those times that in the future I would pass them up with a none-of-my-business attitude, I would have bet my house against it.

17

Today is my son James's bar mitzvah. To say I love him and that I'm proud of him would be a gross understatement. I should also mention that I feel the same way about my son Duke . . . just so years from now there are no issues about Dad. My boys are everything to me. I thank God every day for giving me boys. If I had daughters, I don't think I could handle it. I think about how emotional I am with my sons. I think if I had daughters, I would walk around all day weeping. Too much for me to handle.

Anyway, all I remember from my own bar mitzvah is constantly posing for pictures at tables with my parents' friends. They aren't bad memories, but I wanted to make sure that my son's bar mitzvah was all about him having a fun time. Also, I didn't want to have one of these overblown affairs that cost zillions. Usually they're pompous and boring. Nope, at James's bar mitzvah party it is all about him and his friends. The only adults who are there are immediate relatives and our friends who have a close relationship with James. But the bar mitzvah isn't really relevant to this story, is it? What matters here is that there was literally a ton of delicious candy, cookies, ice cream, and cake. I only know it was there because I paid for it. But I'd pay a heavier price if I ate any of it. Which I don't.

THURSDAY, JUNE 4, 2009
All week, I've been training in the technique of Transcendental Meditation. I go to the center for about an hour a day to be trained by the man in the beige suit with the lightly colored ties. He's excellent. And he wears the same style suit every day. His voice is quite soothing.
"Was it effortless? It was quite delicious, no?"

FRIDAY, JUNE 5, 2009
Today is my forty-seventh birthday. I meditate twice. No cake to celebrate today. Only fruit. It is quite delicious, yes.

MONDAY, JUNE 22, 2009
I'm in New York for three weeks filming *The Bounty* with Jennifer Aniston and Gerard Butler. I've learned that for my sobriety, food has to be wasted.

So last night I went to Fine & Schapiro delicatessen and was just going to get a turkey sandwich, but first I said to the waitress, "Is there anything on your menu that is really great that I should really give a try?" She said something about Latvian steak. I eat steak, I'm not exaggerating, maybe a half a dozen times a year. That's not a lot of steak. And now that I don't eat fast food, I eat burgers probably about the same number of times.

Anyway, I have this steak, and I have some kasha varnishkes (another Jewish dish), some green beans, and a diet cream soda. And I eat about half the steak, then I get it wrapped up. The purpose of getting it wrapped up is not for me to take it home and eat it later, but so that when I walk back to the hotel and see a homeless person, I can give him a steak. The restaurant is obviously going to throw it out— legally, they can give away food that they've cooked in the kitchen but haven't served, but they have to toss any food from the table. So I take it with me, but on my walk back to the hotel, not one homeless person. I've always said that you can't find a homeless person when you really need one.

I've got the leftover steak and I'm going from the hotel to the Russian and Turkish Baths to see a friend. In the car on the way down there, I'm thinking, *They'll drop me off right in front, I won't see a homeless person, and I can't keep it in my locker at the baths; the steak is going to go bad.* So I eat the other half of the steak in the back of the car.

Now I realize for my sobriety, to stay healthy, I have to be wasteful: I have to eat half and throw the other half in the garbage. Can't bring it home, as I may end up eating it. I just have to say no. Especially in L.A., where there's even less chance of seeing a homeless or hungry person from my car on the way home. It's not like there's a park where they all hang out that I can drive by and say, "Hey, who wants this?"

But when I think about it from an ecological standpoint, toss-ing half a steak is not as bad as throwing plastic in the gar-bage that won't biodegrade. It's fine, but that doesn't mean it's not wasteful. But I have to do it, otherwise I'm hurting myself.

TUESDAY, JUNE 23, 2009

I've been eating only fruits and vegetables, all day. Even though it sounds good, having salads and bananas and blueberries all day, I'm starving. I did the forty-five minutes of cardio this morning, which I promised myself I'd do every day since leav-ing Pritikin, and I'm starving. I shower and go up the street to Zabars, and I get egg salad, shrimp salad, whitefish salad, slices of nova lox, cream cheese, and kasha varnishkes. Then I go across the street to H & H Bagels and I get three whole-wheat bagels—oh great, whole wheat, as if that's going to make up for everything else.

I come back to my hotel room, sit down, and I end up eat-ing two of the three bagels and most of the chopped liver (I forgot I also bought chopped liver) and the egg salad. After all that food, of course, I end up feeling sick and bloated. Not nauseous, b-l-o-a-t-e-d. I only drank water with it, not soda. That was my one kindness to myself. I can't go to sleep because I'm so bloated. I wash my clothes.

Folding relaxes me. I'm truly an addict. I forget that. I need to go back to OA. I do well for a while and then I forget. I'm an addict.

I am sitting in an OA meeting in a church basement in New York City. I'm actually feeling a sense of, I don't know . . . warmth. I feel like it's going to work. I'm going to take it seriously. I'm an addict and I need to. The woman running the meeting is very welcoming. It's great to share my problem with a room full of like minds. We read the twelve steps and twelve traditions. I'm so hopeful.

People are straggling in a few minutes late. One of them plops herself down. The only reason I notice her is that she's drinking a giant, sugary Jamba Juice. I'm not allowed to question her. No cross-talk allowed. No asking the woman who is running the meeting to do something about it. I can no longer hear anything being said. It's a giant cup of Jamba Juice. At an OA meeting! My concentration and serenity are gone.

I receive the donation basket. I put in a couple of bucks and pass it to the woman next to me. She reaches into her purse and pulls out some money. She passes the basket on and reaches back in her purse. She's feeling around for something. She finds what she's looking for and smiles. She reaches her other hand in and begins to rip something open. From where I'm sitting, I can see into her purse. She's ripping open a Clif Bar. A Chocolate Chip Clif Bar! I glance over at the woman sipping her Jamba Juice. I laugh and slip out of the meeting.

Sitting outside on the steps of the church, I turn my phone on. OA can be such a bunch of crap. Not OA the program, but most of the people who go to OA. In OA very few people who come in have bottomed out. It's more along the line of, "I heard this is a good place to lose weight." Alcoholism and drug use are always taken seriously. I think A.A. works so well because plenty of those people bottom out. OA will always have its problems because overeating and obesity are hard to take seriously, because society doesn't take them seriously.

Just then my phone rings. It's Susie. I tell her about my overeating last night, how frustrated I feel. "Despite what you think," she says, "you have changed the way you look. You have lowered your footprint. Your breathing isn't heavy and you look healthier. With your short hair and when you wear your glasses, people don't recognize you." She's referring to earlier last night, when I went to see her perform at the Friars Club—before the show people didn't recognize me, and she introduced me as her real husband. Marla has mentioned it to me before that I look different, but I haven't really noticed. I guess with the weights and Pilates and some weight loss, maybe I have changed my personal footprint.

Later that night in my hotel, I'm looking through my notes for this book, and I find a letter. It says "wide awake" on the envelope. When you are in touch with your addiction, your weaknesses, you're wide awake. When you're aware of what you're eating and you're not on autopilot, you're wide awake.

I remember the night I wrote the letter; I had just watched one of my favorite movies, *The Wild Bunch*. At the end of the movie, it's the turn of the century and things are changing. There are two guys still alive from the Wild Bunch—one of

them is on a horse with another group of guys, and the other
is sitting on the ground. The guy on the horse says, "Do you
want to come with us?" The guy on the ground is not sure if
he wants to go, so the guy on the horse says, "It ain't like it
used to be, but it'll do." Which is such simple wisdom: life
changes. I remember thinking, *So I've had a stroke, I'm not as
vibrant as I once was, I'm older. I didn't become a star earlier like
I thought I would. I thought I'd be Eddie Murphy. But it'll do. For
Christ's sake, I've got a great family, I love my job. It'll do.* Here's
the letter I wrote to myself:

Saturday, March 17, 2007, 10:51 p.m.
I'm at the Four Seasons Hotel in San Francisco. Room 902.
I'm with Marla, James, and Duke. They're in the other room
sleeping. I had a session today at Pixar for WALL-E.
The following must be every day: Vegetarian. No sugar.
Exercise, even if it's just for twenty minutes. Sleep at least
seven hours a night. Listen and talk to my family—very im-
portant. Planning and solitude every night before bed and in
morning.
The following should be every day: Laugh. Make love—
idealistic, obviously. Listen to records. Read books. Watch
movies. Go for a walk. Spend some time with my dogs—I
love my dogs. Do the following when you can: Spend time
with friends. Watch sports. Play sports. Read comics. Surf the
internet, when you can. Read magazines and the New York
Times, *when you can.*
Goals: Make good films that people see. Ease their pain
with comedy. Weigh less than 235. Be in excellent physical

health. Be in excellent mental health. Be wise. Be kind. I'm wide awake.

This is from March 2007, two years ago. But it's amazing that I had the same goals and the same game plan to achieve those goals back then. Only now I have added living green to the list. And that's when I realize . . . there is no ending to this story. There is no: "I lost my seventy pounds and my house is completely green." It's an ongoing process; there is no endgame.

It's like success; you think that at some point you make it and then it's easy. Nope. The hard work never goes away. In some ways it's harder. No coasting. I know when I lose weight and get fit it will be hard enough to maintain that, let alone improve. The same with being green. I assume the challenges will just keep on coming. But I hope I'll be up to it.

I won't quit taking the bus. If I take it a couple of times a week, that makes a difference. That's what it's about: just try and make a difference. I've insulated my house, I am putting in a green bathroom, and maybe, someday soon, I'll get my new windows. And with those windows, a divorce.

Truthfully, I know that there is so much more I need to do. I have to keep making the changes. I have to keep going to OA, Jamba Juice or not. I should give myself credit. I've lost over twenty pounds since *Curb* started, and I usually gain ten. Slow and steady, I know, is the way to better health. Keep the weight going down, that's all.

I notice that in the letter I wrote "planning and solitude." I hope I've found some of that with TM. I wonder if, to a degree, there is a version of this letter from two years ago—not written, but perhaps expressed—from two years before that. I know that I've been putting off being healthy for too long. Even before my stroke, I was actively procrastinating. But that story is over. And the new story will be apparent when you see me. Because if I've done these things by then, you'll see a joyful and physically fit person. And you'll see a change in my body of work; I'll be producing things that are good for people, that make people happy. Easing their pain—that's my job. I really look at that as my job. I ease peoples' pain. I know it's a lofty goal, but that's how I feel.

And if there's one thing I've learned in writing this book, why not be lofty? And green? And healthy?

18

I have been in a depression. I did a phone session with my therapist in New York, and he suggested that I see a psychiatrist, someone I've seen before. The last time I saw this psychiatrist was when I was filming *Curb Your Enthusiasm* last season. He was the guy who helped me while he was eating an ice-cream cone.

Today I drive out to Stewart's office in Malibu. His office is in his house, which is at the top of a hill. I realize, as I get to the top of the hill, that I didn't bring his address. My cell phone has no service. So I drive down the hill until I get service, which only happens near the bottom. I call Stewart and he tells me the address. I drive up. I forget the number, so I drive back down again. Once again, I get the address and up I go to his place.

I'm seeing him specifically to go on an antidepressant, or to see if I should. I have never been on an antidepressant in my life. I've been depressed, I've been filled with anxiety, and

I've even had—well, when I was in my twenties—suicidal thoughts. But they weren't serious. I think everyone, when they're younger, thinks, *I'll just kill myself,* whether because of a relationship or something else going on. It's the drama. But even if you're thinking about it, it's serious. The question is, how did I get to this point in my life as an adult, where I'm depressed?

I tell Stewart all the great things that I have, which I won't bother going into here. I tell him I'm depressed. I can't have sex, I feel numb to everything, and when I wake up every morning, I'm filled with a sense of dread. That, to me, is depression. I'm also having trouble sleeping. Can't sleep, can't fuck—what do you do?

Stewart's office consists of a couple of chairs by the pool with an ocean view. I've had sessions in small offices in big cities, some with views and some with no windows. That's what I'm used to. It was weird to be distracted by a grand view of the Pacific. I also kept looking to see if the neighbors were listening. We were talking about my family and this and that. After laying it all out for him, I said, "So what do you think?"

"Well, I think it's your addiction."

"Really? You think it's my food addiction?"

"Yes, and I'll tell you why." And then he tells me that whenever he sees people for the first time, the very first thing they say when they walk into his office is always of great importance. He said that you only find out later why. The first thing I said when I saw him today, when we started our session, was that I'm sober. That I haven't had any cookies, cake, ice cream, or fast food for seven months.

"It's your sobriety," he says. And the reason for this, he tells me, is that I'm dealing with lots of stressful things. Normally I would reach for some food for comfort. A cupcake. And a cupcake would numb me. Well, I have no cupcakes and essentially my tank is on empty. That is why Stewart prescribes Lexapro.

The next morning my wife and I take my son to the bus to go to camp and then I go to my office. I'm working on this book seven days a week now. And no ice cream to make me feel better. I feel like crap. I leave my office to go see a movie and I get some popcorn. I know you don't think it's a big deal to get popcorn, but it's a big deal for me. I don't suck down the popcorn, but I eat most of it, more than I should. It has a ton of salt on it. It makes me feel a little better. Not much. Milk Duds would have done a much better job, but they wouldn't have been worth the guilt. When you go seven full months of being sober, you don't want to ruin it.

I go home and my wife can tell I've had a tough day and is being very supportive. Just being with her and my son makes me feel so much better. Certainly, spending time with my family is better for me than eating ice cream. There are worse things than being addicted to your family. Later my wife goes to visit some friends, and my son Duke sits on my lap downstairs, nestled into me. And we watch *Star Trek*. Suddenly he has this affinity for the old *Star Trek*, so we watch it together. I feel content, full of ease.

● ● ●

At last I finally understand what this book is really about: Everyone who wants to lose weight—or change, but I'm going to go with weight right now—needs an impetus. For an actor it might be, "I have to take my shirt off in this scene." For an actress it might be, "I have to take my shirt off in this scene." Or maybe it's February and you've just binged through the holidays, and you decide, "I want to look good in my bikini this summer." You need an impetus.

My impetus was: I'll write this book. The book meant a deadline, an audience, and real external pressure. A book contract, for sure, would make me lose weight. Little did I know that my impetus would become my albatross. That it would become the thing that created more anxiety and stress, and that it would get worse because I couldn't eat to relieve the stress. But again and again, I did eat.

ooooooooooooooooooooooooooooooooooooooooooooooooooooooooo
ooooooooooooooooooooooooooooooooooooooooooooooooooooooo
ooooooooooooooooooooooooooooooooooooooooooooooooooooooo

Okay, the reason I put the o's here is because something happened, but it wasn't self-inflicted. The x's were for bad and self-inflicted. So tonight, as I'm writing, I start to get a pain in the left side of my lower stomach. It's steadily getting worse. I wake up my wife.

"My side hurts."

"What did you eat?"

"This is not from an upset stomach."

I drive to my local hospital and call my wife to tell her I'm okay. As I check in at the emergency room, the pain is becoming unbearable. Sensing that I'm in great pain, the receptionist hands me three papers to fill out. Lots of details. Fine, that's the system. I fill them out as quickly as I can. She lets me know that someone will be with me soon. There are a few people in the waiting area. On the television is an episode of *Star Trek* that my son and I watched recently. That will be the only calming experience I have for the next hour. One of the people waiting is a guy in his early twenties. By the way, at this point I'm pacing around because the pain is too intense to sit. I start talking to the young guy.

"This is a really good episode. I just saw it recently. Watch this scene; it's crazy." It's the episode "Charlie X," a scene where Lieutenant Uhura is singing a crazy song while Mr. Spock plays some futuristic instrument.

I then think out loud, "How long till they get me? The pain is getting worse."

The young guy asks, "Where's the pain?"

"My stomach."

"Where?"

I lift up my shirt and show him.

"Is the pain in your back, too?"

"Yes."

"It's probably kidney stones. I just had them. If you were bloated, I'd say it's something else."

A door opens and an older nurse calls my name. I thank the guy for his diagnosis. It will be the only one I get at this hospital. She walks me to my room. Well, not my room. It's a room that I'm going to be sharing with a young Hispanic couple and their baby. The girl, who looks pregnant, is lying in the bed. On the foot of the bed is the guy holding the baby. Separating us is a thin curtain. As the nurse pulls the curtain closed, I jokingly say to them, "Don't tell anyone anything, you hear?" I always try being light when things are at their worst.

The nurse asks me some questions, gives me a gown, and leaves without saying anything.

After a few minutes the pain is now quite intense; I walk out into the hall. No one is there. Very softly, I say, "Hello, is anyone here?"

The nurse pops out and brandishes me, "Sir, I need you to go back in your room."

"I'm sorry, I was just wondering . . ."

"Rico, I need your help."

A tall and menacing orderly comes out of another room.

"Rico, have this man go back in his room." Rico looks at me like I'm an escaped mental patient.

"I need you to go back into your room."

"I just wanted . . ."

"Go back in your room."

I go back into my half of the room. I can't lie back on the bed; the pain is too intense. I sit at the foot of the bed rocking. A few minutes later the nurse comes in.

"I need you to lie back on the bed." I lie back.

"Rough night?" I ask.

She doesn't answer. Instead, she yells out, "Rico, I need your help." I really thought Rico would be coming in to tie me down.

"I need you to get his vitals while I do this." "This" meaning putting an IV in my arm. He takes my vitals. I smile at him.

"Rough night?"

No answer. They leave. I don't know what to think. I feel like I'm in a horror movie. I can't tell you at this point if the pain is getting worse or not. It was already so intense, who can tell? I'm rocking back and forth, praying that I won't die. The nurse comes back in, not to check on me, but to get something. While she's there I ask her, "How much longer until a doctor sees me?"

"He's upstairs, and I don't know when he's coming back. There's nothing I can do."

"There's only one doctor and you don't know when he's coming back?"

"Yes." Not "Yes, sorry," or "It's crazy, I know. Just hang tight."

She leaves and I make an attempt to meditate. My fear of death and the following stop me: The baby on the other side of the curtain begins to cry. It seems no one is attempting to soothe it. A woman is brought to the emergency room screaming louder than anything I've ever heard. She is obviously in huge pain. Her screams are so strange that I have no idea what's wrong with her. I keep trying to meditate. Everything seems to get worse—the baby crying, the woman hollering, my pain, my fear, and my frustration. I take all the wires off me. The machine they are attached to starts making a loud beeping noise. I stand up and put my clothes on. I know no one will come in to see what's going on. I walk into the hallway and another nurse stops me.

"Can I help you?"

"I'm leaving."

"Okay?"

"Can you take this off?" Referring to the IV.

"We're very busy and . . ." She looks up at a monitor.

"What's your name?"

"Jeff Garlin."

"You've only been here fifty-three minutes."

"I'm going to go. Would you please take this off?"

She acquiesces with a huff and a puff. She then rips out the IV and haphazardly applies some gauze.

"Wherever you go tonight, you'll end up waiting five hours."

"I'd rather wait five hours anywhere else but here."

I head outside and get in my car. I call my wife, and without too many details, I tell her that I'm going to Cedars-Sinai Medical Center. It's a bit of a drive but I know I'll get much better care there. Actually, I could get better care at a 7-Eleven. Cedars is where both of my boys were born, and I've been in there for numerous reasons including my stroke.

As soon as I walk into the emergency room, it's a different world. The man behind the counter asks me what's wrong. I tell him and he has me sit down. He asks for my information and takes my vitals. As I roll up my sleeve, the gauze that the nurse put on at the previous hospital is covered in blood. After he takes my vitals, I tell him that it's probably kidney stones.

"Oh, my. I'm so sorry. I hear that is very painful. We'll get you taken care of right away."

SYMPATHY!

As I'm waiting, I begin to pace around the waiting area. A security guard asks me if I'm okay.

"My stomach and back are killing me. I think maybe it's kidney stones."

"Really? I hear that's painful. It won't be long before they get you in."

"Thanks."

"Are you a Bulls fan?" I'm wearing a Chicago Bulls sweatshirt. After some more intense pain, pacing, and sports talk, they finally come get me.

Without going into every detail, let me just say that within minutes I'd been given drugs that took away the pain completely, had a CAT scan, and been diagnosed. When I first got to my room, the nurse asked me questions, took my vitals, and inserted an IV. After she put the IV in my arm, she actually said, "Aw, Booh, we'll get you feeling good right away." She called me Booh. I felt like I'd been on a heinous game show and someone was filming my reaction to being treated so wonderfully after my time in hell. Booh. Wow!

Then finally the doctor came in. What a guy.

"Well, you've got a kidney stone that's just about ready to go into your bladder." I think back to that guy in the crappy hospital's waiting room who diagnosed me correctly.

I explained to the doctor (Dr. David Ulick—why not give him some credit) what had happened to me. He was aghast.

"That's terrible. I'm sorry to hear that."

"Well, I just want to thank you for being so kind."

"It's my job. We're all going to be patients someday. I just treat people the way I'd want to be treated. It's my job to make people feel better."

"That's the way I feel. It's my job to ease peoples' pain. They need humor."

"That's a great outlook."

"You, too."

"Thanks."

I would now like to share with you my favorite joke.

A man goes to the doctor. The doctor says, "What can I do for you?"

The man says, "Doctor, I'm so depressed and filled with so much anxiety that I have trouble getting out of bed in the morning. I can't even motivate myself to open the curtains and let some light in my room. I'm filled with so much pain and hopelessness, I don't know what to do."

The doctor says, "I'll tell you what to do. You force yourself to get out of that bed and go see Cocoa the Clown. He's in town now performing. He'll make you laugh and forget about all your problems."

The man says, "But doctor, I am Cocoa the Clown."

When I think back to when I was in the hospital after I had the stroke, I was quite down as I was lying in bed late at night. I couldn't sleep. What would become of me? The only solace I got was from the Cedars-Sinai in-house television channel. It would show old television comedies like *Burns and Allen, Jack Benny,* and *Sergeant Bilko.* I would watch and laugh. Laugh at my darkest moments. As a matter of fact, on one of the Jack Benny shows I watched, Louis Nye guest-starred. It was a great episode, and he and Benny were hilarious. Shortly thereafter, he played my father on *Curb Your Enthusiasm.* He had the funniest line ever on our show. In the episode where we open our restaurant he said, "Boy Cock, Girl Cock, Ee i ee i oh!"

Comedy is very important to me. I'm very proud to be a comedian. Once when I was down and thinking of quitting, I remember watching a broadcast of Bob Newhart speaking at the National Press Club. One of the things that he said was that as a comedian you have a responsibility to keep performing and using your gift. He's right. I have a responsibility to keep going. To ease the pain.

While I was recovering, I would go onstage at the Laugh Factory in L.A., night after night, not having my full skills. It was terrifying, but I kept doing it, every night. And eventually I was good again. Watch the early episodes of *Curb Your Enthusiasm* and you'll see how far I've come. When faced with adversity, I fight it. Yes, I get scared, but I'm lucky. I have the ability to move forward through my fears; I don't get paralyzed by them. Right now I have to face my fears. Not with the kidney stone, which I'm sure, I'll pass in the next few days. But with change.

Remember what I said to my children? Take what you do seriously, but don't take yourself so seriously. It used to be that if you asked me what I do, I'd say, I'm a father, a husband, and a comedian. Now I realize that this is also what I do. Yes, I'm a father, a husband, and a comedian, but one who's conscious about being healthy and green. I can't say that I'm healthy and green. That would be too simple and a bunch of bullshit. I'll try to keep my footprint light. I'm conscious. I'm wide awake. I'm done with this book. I'm off to plant a tree.